THE MANHOOD TEST

By

William A. "Tony" Lavelle

Gallantry Group Press
Sacramento, California
www.gallantrypress.com

THE MANHOOD TEST

Copyright © 2012 by William A. "Tony" Lavelle

The publication is designed to provide education and entertainment about the subject matter covered. Because of the dynamic nature of the Internet, any web addresses or links contained in this book may have changed since publication and may no longer be valid.

The views expressed in this work are solely those of the author.

PUBLISHED BY:

Gallantry Group Press
1900 Vallejo Way
Sacramento, California USA
95818-3845
916-416-6008
www.gallantrypress.com
Publisher@gallantrypress.com

For reviews & comments direct to the author: gallantry@lanset.com

Covers & interior designed by William A. "Tony" Lavelle

ISBN: 978-0-9839635-1-6

Printed in the United States of America
FIRST EDITION, APRIL 2012

Dedication

I dedicate this book to the millions of Men out there who get little recognition for properly handling their responsibilities every day —doing what is expected of a Man—as a mature and responsible Adult, a loyal and involved Citizen, a loving and faithful Husband, and a patient and caring Father.

Thank you, gentlemen, for steadfastly and courageously, conducting your lives as Men.

*"It takes more courage to reveal insecurities
than to hide them,
more strength to relate to people
than to dominate them,
more 'manhood' to abide by thought-out principles
rather than blind reflex.
Toughness is in the soul and spirit,
not in muscles and an immature mind."*

— Alex Karras, a former football player, professional wrestler, and actor

Contents

Preface

Instead of becoming Men when they reach the age of adulthood, our boys remain sniveling, whining little babies. Under our very noses, our young adult males are failing in great numbers to reach Manhood. Much more troubling is that our society is fast becoming a nation of castrated eunuchs.* Our boys today are too lost, lazy, and ignorant to even realize their sole purpose in life is to become a Man—a mature and responsible Adult, a loyal and involved Citizen, a loving and faithful Husband, and a patient and caring Father.

I wrote this book because I found out that Manhood is declining. More and more of our boys are unable, unwilling, or just uninterested in becoming a Man. I see more males dropping out of high school, going to jail, doing drugs, making bastard children, or just laying around their parents' homes, playing video games, smoking weed, and screaming and whining at their moms to hurry up with their dinner. Another reason I wrote this book is because I have a crazy idea that could just solve this problem. We can save our boys by, together, teaching them to be happy and successful Men.

* "Eunuch" is the job title of an ancient career field employing only castrated males. Eunuchs were employed as special guards in a royal palace. A eunuch's job was to protect "access" to the King's private harem of concubines. The King was the only male allowed to have "access" to the girls in his harem. Because the young women were the most beautiful and seductive in the Kingdom, the King could not take any chances. He had every eunuch's balls cut off to guarantee no "access" by any man but the King. Before the rookie eunuch could start his new job, the "King's Castrator" has one of his assistants, using a large pair of pliers, stretch tight the new eunuch's scrotum. The elongated sack was then sliced off with a large knife, or chopped off with an ax.

Some eunuch trivia—when newly hired eunuchs were castrated, their severed scrotums, containing the removed testicles, were placed on a tray and displayed for the King as proof they were ready to go to work. The term "eunuch" is used informally to describe a male who is ineffective, weak, and/or cowardly. Hence, my use of this term.

Acknowledgements

I am extremely grateful to the hundreds of women I interviewed for this project, all of whom shared their valuable time and intimate feelings with me. I learned so much, especially that women are tired and frustrated from having the responsibility forced upon them to train boys to be decent Men. They, in reality, expect us Men to take charge and be responsible for instructing our boys how to be Men: the mature and responsible adult, loyal and involved citizen, loving and faithful husband, and patient and caring father.

> "I'm mad as hell, and I'm not going to take this anymore!"
> — Howard Beale, movie Network

Women deserve to fall in love with a good Man. They are absolutely fed up with having to kiss so many toads just to find one gallant prince. This book will help them to find that perfect Man to marry, as they so well deserve.

"I want a man—fully trained and ready to marry—to keep me happy,
making me feel deeply loved and genuinely appreciated.
If my man keeps me happy, then it is so easy
for a good woman keep her man happy.
All they really want from us to be happy is sex, food and toys.
So, after I give him his medicine,
I make my Man a big sandwich or a nice steak.
If he has done an especially good job by me,
I buy him some new toys to play with.
All guys love new toys. I don't care how old they are.
It's a win-win for both of us."
— Jackie S.

Introduction

In my college advanced prose style class, I learned a writer's technique called "confiteri," a Latin term meaning "to confess." My professor said that readers will be a bit more forgiving of an author's occasional prose or grammar error if that author "confesses" in advance that he is not the greatest writer in the world, and asks for the reader's forgiveness. This technique works only if the story can hold the reader's interest in spite of any flaws in the book. The professor said to be careful, too many errors may cause the reader to become distracted by the writer's "subliterate diction" and "Neanderthal writing style." This is my first book. It has taken me four years to write it. Please forgive me as I am sure you will find something "subliterate" or "Neanderthal."

With that said, I remain optimistic that I wrote this book well enough to hold your interest in the topic, and that you will clearly understand the problem as well as my solution. This book is about the decline of manhood and how to fix it, helping our boys become Men.

PROBLEM: boys failing to become men at 18 years old. No clear definition of what it means to be a Man, nor how a boy can reach Manhood.

SOLUTION: Define what a Man is. Explain how a boy can reach Manhood, becoming a mature and responsible Adult, a loyal and involved Citizen, a loving and faithful Husband, and a patient and caring Father.

Check out the appendixes at the end first. The bulk of this book explains what they are for.

CHAPTER 1

What's the Problem With Our Boys?

"The belief in a supernatural source of evil is not necessary;
men alone are quite capable of every wickedness."
— Joseph Conrad, Novelist, 1911

"Man, when perfected, is the best of animals,
but, when separated from law and justice, he is the worst of all."
— Aristotle

I will call him Rick. He is tall and handsome, a blond, white, middle class, soon to be 26 year old male living in Northing, California. He is a high school graduate with about three semesters of underwhelming ("B" to "C" average) community college performance under his belt. Rick's mom just sold a prosperous women's fitness center. She is a 2nd degree black belt in judo and has her masters in English. Rick's dad is a successful businessman who now works for a big hotel chain. Mom and Dad have been divorced for 20 years. Rick was arrested by the police a few days after his 18th birthday for possession of a small amount of weed. A few years later he was busted for DUI where weed was the intoxicant. Rick drifted from low paying job to low paying job, quitting or getting fired from every one of them.

I tell you this because today, 14 September 2011, Rick is homeless, jobless and penniless. His parents finally had to throw him out a few years ago, otherwise he would have just hibernated when not playing video games. When he was 19 I had him all set up to join the Air Force Reserves as a flying air crewman/load master on the C-117 transport out of Travis AFB. He met the squadron chief master sergeant. The chief liked Rick immediately and welcomed him to join the squadron. Rick would have traveled the world, earning at least $50,000.00 a year. Plus free medical, and free apartment, free uniforms, and a $60K+ College scholarship. Rick walked away from it saying, "I am worried how the military would change me." Now that he is desperate for anything, no one, the Air Force, and not even the Army, will take Rick because of his criminal record. Rick was frustrated, blaming his father for not telling him what to do. Grrrr! I wanted to smack this kid.

There are millions of boys like Rick out there, wandering and lost. They can't even make it to the first step of becoming a Man, adulthood. That's the problem, Manhood is declining. Rick's generation is the worst I have ever seen. I thought the problem was just here in America. I found it the same in Europe, Australia, even Japan with its "Grass-eating Boys."

Our youngest male adults are failing. "...many of the social problems of our day—plummeting morality, rising crime, violence, abuse, reckless pleasure-seeking—spring from the soil of direction less, disconnected sons." (LEWIS)

"Once-noble imagines of masculinity have now been replaced by images of men behaving badly ... or incompetently ... of both. Manhood is no longer a unique calling; it's now seen more as a problem to overcome." (LEWIS)

My name is Tony Lavelle. As a military Man, I devoted most of my adult life to serving my country, much of that time leading, training and mentoring the young men and women under my command. As a soldier, then civilian, I lived and worked for over 12 years in about 20 countries in Europe and Asia. I have traveled in another 50 or so nations, on every continent but Antarctica. I discovered the best part of living in or visiting a foreign land was studying, and mingling, with the local indigenous humans. I seem to have an aptitude for learning some of the local language and customs, a gifted skill that opens doors for me to enjoy their culture up close. I can't tell you how often I was blessed with the opportunity to just sit quietly in a home in a faraway foreign land, sharing a meal, or just observing the family living their everyday lives. From my observations, I realized that all human families are the same when it comes to their hopes, loves, and desires. Realizing I could study humans as an academic pursuit, I decided to put to embark on a my final career as a newly minted scientist in the contemporary field of applied cultural anthropology. My job now, in the simplest of terms, is to find problems faced by Homo Sapiens, and fix them. I did not realize it at the time, but in 1997, I discovered the phenomenon of our directionless and disconnected sons while an adjunct professor at California State University in Sacramento. (CSUS)

I observed male students, in small groups, in every class, sitting in the back of the classroom doing nothing—not participating in the lectures, not doing homework, and not taking the exams. I had about a half a dozen of what I call "rocks" in every one of my classes.

I had been in the cloistered order of military service for the last 26 years, surrounded by highly trained, extremely motivated, hardworking, young men. Discovering in our colleges this type of slothful male, wasting expensive university resources, was new to me. Eventually curiosity caused me to ask the obvious questions. I woke up one of my "rocks," named Justin, to explain the trend.

- "So, what's your major?" I asked a 20 year old sophomore in his 4th semester at CSUS.
- "I dunno," he answered groggily because I was disturbing his nap.
- "Well, what do you want to do when you finish college?" I asked.
- "I have no idea," he said in a clueless tone.
- Then I asked, "What's your GPA?"
- "About a 1.6."
- "1.6. That's about a D+ grade point average. I bet your parents are proud of you."
- "My dad is pissed."
- "Well, why are you here wasting your time, my time, and your

dad's money?"

• "My dad said I had to either go to work, go in the military, or go to college. I didn't want to work. And the military is too much work. So I'm here."

• "Since you're not studying or doing any homework, what do you do with your time?" I asked.

• "Mostly, I just, you know, hang out and stuff, in my parents' basement. I like to eat, drink beer, smoke weed, and play video games. My mom feeds me and does my laundry. I can live free, doing what I want, when I want."

The "rocks" in my other classes had the same story. I started researching this phenomenon. I discovered a trend, over the last 30 years; the maturity level of young adult males has been dropping. Our culture is in deep trouble, and that the heart of its trouble is our loss, as a culture and society, of the vision of Manhood. The root of the problem is our gender-neutral culture. "Our ... sons ... are growing up in an increasingly feminized world." (LEWIS)

What I think happened to American manhood. I believe our great nation is secretly suffering from a disease I will politely call, "P-Syndrome," or "PS" for short. P-Syndrome induces males— well into their 30s—to display behavior that is dishonorable, cowardly, spineless, lazy, whiny, or simply unbecoming a man. My hypotheses as to the root cause of P-Syndrome is the predominating philosophy and influential lifestyle of my generation—the "baby boomers."

They were "...born in America after the troop demobilization at the end of WWII (1945-65); ... member(s) of the 'me generation' who's responsible for codifying the double-standard in nuisance statutes, for indicting the security and safety of their stable society, for warranting emotional rationalization as a conclusion for debate, for casting aspersions (SIC) upon traditional values without ameliorating them, and other hackneyed mainstays of the counter cultural revolution. These narcissistic BABY BOOMERs, or simply 'boomers', believe that the world began with their birth (and will end with their death), and that they invented wild sex, mind-altering drugs, loud music, lewd dancing, tender words, ridiculous fashions, noble causes, and the "generation gap" ... and like all other egomaniacal solipsists (egoistically self-absorbed), their pathetic claim to individuality is embarrassingly meretricious (gaudy and false) and jejune (immature and childish)." (MIL TERMS B-BRAvO)

> "P-Syndrome is a disease
> that induces males—well into their 30s—to display behavior
> that is dishonorable, cowardly, spineless, lazy, whiny,
> or simply unbecoming a man."
> — William Lavelle

The first strain of PS was cultivated as we boomers came into parenthood. Our mantra was "sex, drugs, and roll and roll." It was a "far out" and "groovy" time to "tune in, turn on, and drop out, man." We spent the day getting stoned, listening to Pink Floyd and Jimi Hendrix. We believed "never trust anyone over 30," and don't be a slave doing "the man's" work. We had no need to learn a work ethic anymore because we had "free love" and "spare change." We invented welfare and food stamps.

I lived on both sides of the tracks at different points in my life. I started as a soldier, and then become a hippie boomer engaging in sex, drugs and rock and roll. Then, I went back to the cloistered order of the military because I found a rush in being a warrior. As a hippie warrior, I agree with what was said above of many, but not all, of the boomers. Not all boomers were hippies. But, we were a demographic juggernaut, and still are, as the curtain opens on our final act as America's largest group of senior citizens.

From American history, we learn that millions immigrated here to build a better life, provide more opportunities for their families, and prepare their children for adulthood. By hard work, willpower, and self-motivation, each generation of Americans was able to achieve that upward mobility mission. After World War 2, the baby boomers came along and undid centuries of parental success. My fellow hippies created a paradigm shift in our cultural norms by moving away from the protestant work ethic, "A view of life that promotes hard work and self-discipline as a means to material prosperity. It is called Protestant because some Protestant groups believe that such prosperity is a sign of God's grace." (PROTESTANT)

The hippies moved us away from the norm of "it takes a village" to train a child for adulthood and marriage to "only the parents can train their spoiled brats for adulthood."

The boomer generation was the first to excessively pamper their children. It was the first time spanking and other forms of corporal punishment were considered a social taboo. Compounding the problem, boomer children, now parents, continue to perpetuate and exacerbate the problem by infecting the newest generation of young American adults with P-Syndrome. They blindly gratify their children's every little whim, denying the little brats nothing. Author Robert Heinlein said it best, "Don't handicap your children by making their lives too easy." Too late. Our newest adults struggle and many fail to achieve successful adulthood. More importantly, that malfunction translates into a weaker, more dysfunctional, American society.

Don't believe me? Answer this question. What percent of American, middle-class, 18 year old males are fully prepared to leave the nest and step out on their own, as mature, responsible adults, with a clear plan of action for the first four to eight years of their adult lives? In doing field research for this book, I asked several hundred adults that question. Their reply—less than 5% of boys are ready for Adulthood at 18. While there is no hard science to support what looks like a trend to me, how did over 95% of the Adults I interviewed give me the same —less than 5%? I can only say that they knowingly or subconsciously realize the problem is that bad, that the maturity level of our youngest adults is awful and worrisome. Especially for the boys.

Still don't think we spoil kids rotten? If you are a baby boomer, what did you have in your bedroom when you were a kid? I was 10 in 1962; I shared a room with my little brother in a middle-class home in Sacramento. In our room, we each had a bunk bed, night stand and light, writing table and chair, and a chest of drawers. We shared a clock radio, a poster of the solar system on the wall, and a toy box full of matchbox cars, toy guns, and green army men. We were happy campers. We were in our rooms for sleeping, dressing, and homework. The rest of the day was outside until the street lights came on.

A maximum security prisoner in our state penitentiary spends 23 hours per day in his cell. He gets one hour of outside time per 24 hours. My 16 year old nephew ignorantly presumed the prisoners lucky to be able to stay in their "rooms" undisturbed. My nephew's bedroom suite comes with a private bath, queen-size bed, 46 inch flat screen TV, satellite television, DVR, personal computer, laptop computer, high-speed internet, a Sony Play Station, PSP, iPod, iPhone, and subscriptions to Netflix for DVDs and internet streaming video. His mom does his laundry and cleans his room. Now, the spoiled brat has been whining to his mommy because she will not buy him a microwave and small refrigerator for his "suite." He said he hates that his mom makes him get out of his room and go outside every day. He thinks 23 hours a day in his room is perfect. What an immature, sniveling little baby. One of those toads a girl will have to kiss as she searches for her perfect Man, her prince.

Can we now agree there exists a problem? Our boys are struggling to become men and adults. Males fail to pass the manhood tests listed in this book all the time. And they go on with their lives thinking they are men. Men can be bad. Of the two genders on our species, we males are by far the leading troublemakers. Just how bad are human males right now? On this planet, males run the world. There are only 19 female heads of state out of 192 members of the United Nations. I try to refrain from using the word "Men" because those males who perpetrated the injustices around the world are not men.

It's a debated axiom in anthropology that because male humans have a penis, we are in charge of nearly everything: nearly every country, every corporation, and every university, court, legislature, and military on the planet. Sociologists and anthropologists can agree that our gender is perfectly suited for world and gender domination. We are physically bigger than women are. Males tend to be more aggressive, violent, ruthless, merciless, cruel, malevolent, and homicidal than human females. And of course, let us not forget we males are the only gender equipped with the necessary penis.

When I think of the terrible cruelty males, not men, inflict on other humans, I associate that bad behavior with words like genocide, weapons of mass destruction, rape, slavery, sexual predator, murder, war, domestic violence, kidnapping, arson, terrorism, child molester, serial killer, pimping, human trafficking, death squads, and torture. In modern history, I have never heard of a female head-of-state perpetrating mass rape or genocide on her people. I am sure there must have been one bad woman in charge somewhere.

The track record of the males in charge of America includes record unemployment, greed from selling billions in bad home loans, record deficits, and millions of American families losing their homes. And, of course, almost 5,000 dead and over 30,000 wounded Americans in two undeclared wars of questionable value in defending our Constitution against all enemies foreign and domestic. I needlessly lost friends and comrades.

We males beat our women, rape them, enslave them, torture them, and kill them. In parts of Africa, we even cut off the woman's vagina because the men in that part of the world decided that their women must never enjoy sex else they turn into whores. Those African women are indoctrinated by their males to willingly endure the lifelong pain to remain members in good standing of their tribe.

In some parts of the world, a man can kill his wife or daughter if she is raped, seen driving a car, or seen not covering her face with a veil. He can sell his daughters into slavery and prostitution. In half the world, men can still marry more than one woman.

Women are bought, sold, and traded like livestock as indentured servants and sex slaves.

Statistics—males not operating like Men:

- In Africa, in 2008, an invading army systematically raped over 30,000 women as a part of their conquest. (DR CONGO)
- One in every four women ... will experience domestic violence in her lifetime. (DOMESTIC)
- One in six women ... has experienced an attempted or completed rape. (DOMESTIC)
- About 32% of all male students in the United States fail to graduate from high school. 43% of black and Hispanic males do not graduate. (UNDERSTANDING HIGH SCHOOL)
- Boys who witness domestic violence twice as likely to abuse women and children when they become adults. (DOMESTIC)
- America is just 5% of the world population and has 25% of the world's prisoners; over 2 million American males are incarcerated, about 1% of adults in the U.S. resident population. 7,225,800 adults (93% males) were under correctional supervision (probation, parole, jail, or prison) in 2009—about 3.1% of adults in the U.S. resident population. (INCARCERATION)
- More young adult males are entering prison. More juveniles are being tried and sentenced as adults because of the seriousness of their crimes. The United States incarcerates more of its youth than any other country in the world. (INCARCERATION)

Summary of the problem.

- Our boys are failing in greater numbers to become Men and achieve Manhood.
- Baby boomers caused the problem.
- P-Syndrome is a disease that infects boys, making it nearly impossible for them, unassisted, to become a Man, an Adult, a Citizen, a Husband, and a Father.

Nearly 80% of Americans are unhappy with government. It will get far worse if we do nothing. By 2020 we will have elected a boy as President. President Knucklehead, the idiot son of rich 1%er.

Daddy bought this eunuch's election like Daddy did for everything else. Even got his son out of jail for attempted rape and drug use. But, the sheep we call voters elected this dumb ass as the leader of the free world.

Sound like a nightmare? President Knucklehead? Can you imagine what an embarrassment America will be to the world with President Knucklehead in charge?

I have a plan to fix this. Read on.

CHAPTER 2

HOW TO HELP BOYS BECOME MEN

*"The lack of emotional security of our American young people is due, I believe,
to their isolation from the larger family unit.
No two people—no mere father and mother—as I have often said,
are enough to provide emotional security for a child.
He needs to feel himself one in a world of kinfolk, persons of variety in age and temperament,
and yet allied to himself by an indissoluble bond which he cannot break if he could,
for nature has welded him into it before he was born. "
– Pearl S. Buck, writer (1892-1973)*

How do we fix this problem? I have a solution. But, it will be a tough sell to those who do not comprehend the magnitude of the P-Syndrome infection. Applied Anthropology is that part of our discipline that hunts for human problems, and tries to fix them. This is my attempt at accomplishing the applied anthropology mission. I think I found a problem so big it impacts our very culture.

Here is my plan.

1. Acknowledge this is a serious problem—the state

of Manhood in our culture is on the decline. It will continue to fall unless we, as a nation, with the willpower to make change, fix it.

2. *Clearly define what a Man is and how to achieve Manhood.*
3. *Reset the legal age for males back to 21 years old.*
4. *Bring back the social norm of "It takes a village to raise a child."*
5. *Ritualize Manhood and Manhood training in our culture.*
6. *Post High School, Continue Uninterrupted Manhood Training.*
7. *Create a National Elder Corps (NEC) Program.*
8. *Test all the males over 18 immediately!*

Some of you will think this a brilliant plan, some will think I am full of shit, and others will not care. To do what I propose will take courage and willpower. My solution should be undertaken in baby steps. Start with:

STEP ONE — Acknowledge the Problem

The first part of my solution to the declining state of Manhood is to acknowledge the problem; to recognize that the state of manhood in our culture is on the decline, and it will continue to decline unless we, as a nation—together—fix the problem.

The maturity level of our boys has been dropping since the 1960s. Our young adult aged males are infected with P-Syndrome, which is castrating them from passing the first test of Manhood—becoming a mature and responsible Adult.

STEP TWO — Define Man

Definition of a Man is: "A male who handles all his business—his duties and responsibilities—
• as a mature and responsible Adult,
• an involved and loyal Citizen,
• a loving and faithful Husband,
• and a patient and caring Father."

The Manhood equation:

Adult + Citizen + Husband + Father = A Man.

"Define a simple, easy to understand definition of manhood
that any male can achieve if they want it." — Bennett

There are four primary duties/areas of responsibility for a Man:

1. Adult (mature and responsible)
2. Citizen (loyal and involved)
3. Husband (loving and faithful)
4. Father (patient and caring)

Each one of those areas has a specific test the male must pass
to progress to greater responsibilities. The first one being the
Adult Manhood Test at age 18 (Appendix 3) to achieve manhood
status. Within a year or two, the new man must pass the Citizen
Manhood Test (Appendix 5), and the Husband and Father Tests
(Appendixes 9 and 11) when he reaches those milestones in his
life. For a boy to become an adult, he must pass Manhood Test
#1 — Adult.

Before the grammar police arrest me, to emphasize their critical
importance, I will use uppercase for words I consider proper
rather than common nouns: Man, Men, Wife, Adult, Citizen,
Husband, Father, Manhood, Manhood Test, and Elder.

STEP THREE — Reinstate the age of adulthood to 21.

Make the legal age 21.

*"If I was in charge, I would make the legal age 30 years old for you
bad boys; and at least 25 for you young foolish girls.
We women are not all sugar and spice princesses, you know.
Maybe 30 is too low for some of you." — Jackie S.*

The science seems to support my rollback of the legal age,
suggesting that males at 18 are still kids, and are not yet ready
to step out as mature and responsible Adults. A boy at 18 is still

an adolescent with a mind of mush. No other animal, not even the other primates, go through adolescence. That time period between puberty and the attainment of adult stature turns out to be something uniquely human. What possible advantage does adolescence confer on humans in the battle for survival? To the contrary, skipping the teens would appear to be an advantage in the survivability of parents! One guess is that adolescence—all 8 or so years of it—is required for the development of the complex social skills needed by adults. (BOGIN)

Adolescence is the time between the beginning of sexual maturation (puberty) and adulthood. It is a time of psychological maturation, which a person becomes "adult-like" in behavior. Adolescence is considered to be the period between ages 13 and 20. It is viewed as a transitional period whose chief purpose is the preparation of children for adult roles. (LARSON) The adolescent experiences not only physical growth and change, but also emotional, psychological, social, and mental change and growth. (PUBERTY) Furthermore, the human brain is not fully developed by the time a person reaches puberty. Between the ages of 10 and 25, the brain undergoes changes that have important implications for behavior. The media often proclaims that the problem behaviors of adolescents are causing the downfall of civilization. It is important to remember that most of these behaviors fade over time. (STEINBERG)

In light of the fact that most injuries sustained by adolescents are related to risky behavior (car crashes, alcohol, unprotected sex), much research has been done on adolescent risk taking, particularly on whether and why adolescents are more likely to take risks than adults. Behavioral decision making theory says that adolescents and adults both weigh the potential rewards and consequences of an action. However, research has shown that adolescents seem to give more weight to rewards, particularly social rewards, than do adults. (ALBERT)

Changes in the socio-emotional system at puberty may promote reckless, sensation seeking behavior in early and middle adolescence, while the regions of the prefrontal cortex that govern cognitive control continue to mature over the course of adolescence and into young adulthood. This temporal gap between the increase in sensation seeking around puberty and the later development of mature self-regulatory competence may combine to make adolescence a time of inherently immature judgment. Despite the fact that in many ways adolescents may appear to be as intelligent as adults, their ability to regulate their (reckless and negligent) behavior in accord with these advanced intellectual abilities is more limited. (STEINBERG, LAWRENCE)

The evidence is strong that the brain does not cease to mature until the early 20s in those relevant parts that govern impulsivity, judgment, planning for the future, foresight of consequences, and other characteristics that make people morally culpable. (GUR)

Business has known for years that young male adults are idiots. Auto insurance companies charge higher premiums on male drivers under 25 than they do females. Car rental companies will not rent to any male under 25. Boys under 21 were having such a hard time behaving themselves while drinking, in the 1980s, the federal government threatened to cut off funds to any state that did not raise the legal drinking age from 18 to 21.

As we start curing our boys of P-Syndrome, and they begin to mature, we can always rollback to 18. But, until we fix this, 21 should be the minimum legal age. Maybe 25 for the next 5 to 10 years?

STEP FOUR – "It takes a village to raise a child."

"It takes a whole village to raise a child."
— African Proverb

Bring back the social norm of "It takes a village to raise a child" that the boomers got rid of. We are of the opinion that the parents alone are raising the child or sometimes even one parent alone (usually the mother) while the other one works long hours, goes off to war, or just runs away. Since the baby boomers took over, we parent alone. We raise our children alone, an exhausting and, many times, unproductive method of child rearing. In traditional societies, it is true that people co-sleep, breast feed much longer, and wear their babies all the time. But when the village raises the child there are grandparents, aunts, neighbors, and older children to share the parenting. In our society, if the mother cannot do it all, all of the time, we look down on her. Alternately, if she isn't willing to just leave her baby with some stranger in order to get a break, we look down on her. (IT TAKES VILLAGE TO RAISE A CHILD)

While I am not a Hillary Clinton fan, I thought her book nailed it. In "It Takes a Village: And Other Lessons Children Teach Us," published in 1996, Mrs. Clinton presents her vision for the children of America, focusing on the impact individuals and groups outside the family have, for better or worse, on a child's well-being, advocating a society which meets all of a child's needs. The "It takes a village" child rearing philosophy means that every person in a community has a vested interest in seeing to it that every child is well cared for, well educated, and well raised. The best way for a child to be well cared for, educated, and raised is for every adult in that child's community to have a active role in that child rearing process.

In the 21st century, when the extended family that used to be a youngster's loving village are so far away from one another, the call is out to neighbors, teachers, coaches, religious leaders, to be members of the village. Under this model, all adults have the fiduciary community responsibility to train children to be mature and responsible Adults and loyal and involved Citizens. Men are the primary trainers of boys. The women, of course, have the responsibility for training girls to become Women. My focus in this book is the boys. One or two parents can't teach a boy everything. Boys need continuous Adult supervision and mentoring by Men if our boys are to become men themselves.

It will take a village to raise a child.

STEP FIVE — Ritualize Manhood and Manhood Training.

Establish a national rite-of-passage program. Make the passing of each test, each step of Manhood extraordinary with a special ceremony. A rite-of-passage is a human ritual that marks a person's progress from a social status, such as a boy graduating to Manhood, by passing his Adult Manhood Test. Rites-of-passage are often simple to elaborate initiation ceremonies; baptism, confirmation, and Bar Mitzvah are considered important rites-of-passage for people of their respective religions.

Becoming a Man must be a universal goal all boys strive for. We should establish distinctive rite-of-passage ceremonies as a life goal all boys would be eager to undertake. We must make the path to manhood special, challenging, and exciting for our boys. If you want to be "cool," then you will want to become a Man as soon as possible, because if you are 18 or older, what would we call you if cannot call you a man? A baby? A loser? A pansy?

Primary education must incorporate a formal Manhood training curriculum starting no later than kindergarten or first grade. The training objective is to prepare the boys to master the Adult and Citizen skills (Appendixes 1 and 4), so they can pass the corresponding tests.

The first test of manhood is Manhood Test #1 — Adult (Appendix 3). The boys take that test at 18 years old.

Schools team with the parents and the Elders (see step 7) to prepare boys for their first test that will make them Men, and mature responsible Adults. The training must start as soon as boys are out of diapers, and continue until they can pass all the tests of Manhood.

There are four tests of Manhood and rite-of-passage ceremonies: Adult, Citizen, Husband, and Father. The skills of each and the tests are easy to find in the Appendix section of this book.

STEP SIX — Post High School, Continue Uninterrupted Manhood Training.

The Masai of Africa start training their boys for Manhood when they are 6 years old. Masai males become Men at about 14. They stay in the Manhood training program their entire lives, moving from boy to Man to Elder and Chief. Our training program must be as robust as the Masai have. I designed a chart of a typical male's progress through his life, and the tests of manhood he will take (Appendix 1).

After passing the Adult test, our new young men must continue to train to pass the manhood test for citizenship, then eventually marriage and fatherhood. That training and testing continues lifelong. Eventually the Man, as he gets older, will move from student to teacher and Elder, the next step.

STEP SEVEN — National Elder Corps (NEC)

The NEC—the cornerstone organization supporting the "It takes a village" model. The Corps is composed of Men and Women, local community adults called "Elders." For the Men, the Corps would be mature Men in good standing in the community, who would work jointly with parents and teachers. All Elders are trained, and granted local authority to supervise, train, and mentor all boys and young Men they come across.

The Father is the primary Manhood skills instructor for his son. He and the Elder Corps work together to train all boys in our schools and community. The Corps will administer the Manhood tests and host the rite-of-passage ceremonies. I envision all Elders would carry a hard wood staff as their badge of office much as the Masai Men all carry a herding stick. Should some boys or young men act up in the schools or neighborhoods, the Elders would "handle it." No boy would be able to anything stupid because the Elders would be everywhere "mentoring" him.

Another way of understanding what an Elder is: in martial arts, the Elder would be the master, the sensei, with the black belt. A village Elder in a Masai village trains boys for manhood and is a village supervisor.

The first mission for the Corps is to carry out the last step of my plan.

STEP EIGHT — Test All Males Immediately

Every male, 18 and older, the Elders must administer Manhood Test #1 — Adult (Appendix 3) to them. We need a clear picture as to the scope of the problem; how badly has P-Syndrome infected our males? Who is a Man, and what male is still a boy?

* * * * *

A Man, Defined

**"A Man is a male who handles all his business,
his primary duties and responsibilities,
as a mature and responsible Adult,
an involved and loyal Citizen,
a loving and faithful Husband,
and a patient and caring Father."**

— William Lavelle

That's it. My eight steps to fix that problem. Let the whining and sniveling begin. It seems to be human nature to complain. But, it takes genuine courage to put that solution on the table to be challenged as I have done in this book. Understand, my solution is merely one Man's idea, put forward in the absence of any better suggestion. Accomplishing my solution will take willpower, leadership, and teamwork. I doubt America will do it because it is far too easy to stand on the side lines and complain than to step on the field and work.

Each one of those four duties can be tested. There are four tests of manhood—Adult, Citizen, Husband, and Father. The list of skills for each duty, and the tests, are easy to find in the Appendix section of this book.

If he passes all the tests, that Man has earned his place in the Brotherhood of Men. If he fails any test, then he is not a man. I am sure you can think of some names we use to label males who are over 18, but not men. P-Syndrome is actually a global epidemic. In German, they call males who flunk the tests of Manhood "Memme," a wimp or candy-ass.

Just a week ago, my friends in Japan told me that even in their country P-Syndrome is becoming infectious. Japanese women now complain about the difficulty in finding good Men to marry. In Japan, males who flunk the test are called "Soshoku Danshi," literally translated as "grass-eating (baby) boys. So named for their lack of interest in sex and their preference for quieter, less competitive (lazy) lives. Currently, 60 percent of men in their early twenties, and at least 42 percent of Japanese males, aged 23 to 34 consider themselves grass-eating men.

As the population of grass-eating males increase, there is a corresponding increase in "meat-eating girls," "Niku Shokukei Joshi," women in their twenties who now tend to be aggressive toward men, love, sex, and marriage. Meat-eating girls approach men because the grass-eating males are no longer approaching women.

I have explained the problem. I defined what a Man is, and a course of action a boy can follow to achieve Manhood. Over the next few chapters, I will examine each duty in greater detail. I will provide the skills checklist, and the Manhood test for each duty, starting with the first step to Manhood—becoming a mature and responsible Adult.

CHAPTER 3

Mature & Responsible Adult

"For only as we ourselves, as adults, actually move and have our being in the state of love,
can we be appropriate models and guides for our children.
What we are teaches the child far more than what we say,
so we must be what we want our children to become."
— *Joseph Chilton Pearce, writer*

Can we say, are you comfortable in saying, that boys are achieving Adulthood, becoming Men later in life, if at all? Eighteen years old is the legal age in America. On his 18th birthday, we must legally say the boy is now an Adult and Citizen, and by default, a Man. By our social norm that new Man takes his place in society as a mature and responsible Adult, and a loyal and involved Citizen. But, don't forget, he is still an adolescent. His brain is not yet running on all cylinders. He still has another seven or so years before his brain can run at full power.

None the less, our culture states that at 18, ready or not, the boy is an Adult. To become a mature and responsible Adult, a boy must master the skills needed of an Adult, then pass his first test of manhood (Appendix 3). Remember my definition of a Man: A male handing his business has an adult, citizen, husband, and father. A boy's journey to Manhood begins when he starts to learn the skills of Adulthood and Citizenship.

Over the next five chapters, I have broken down, with a chapter each, the four duties of a Man. I say five chapters because I include in chapter 5 the "Pre-Husband" checklist and test. The pre-husband period begins when the Man begins his search for a good woman to be his Wife. It ends when he is engaged to be married. The Pre-Husband Test is unique in that it is administered by the Woman contemplating marrying that Man. She uses that test to help her decide to say yes or no to his proposal of marriage.

In each chapter, I will introduce and explain the skills that must be mastered in each of the duties, followed by the test. There are four tests of manhood over a man's life. The first being Manhood, Test #1 — Adult. Appendix 1 breaks down when each test must be taken. Do you follow me? First, I gave you the list of skills for each duty, then I explain each skill. Finally comes the applicable Manhood test. Potty training is the very first skill a boy must master on his journey to manhood. Once he is potty trained, keep the training going.

The military had an outstanding system for training soldiers. The first step is a list of tasks to perform or skills to master. That's followed by testing to ensure the soldier has mastered those skills. The skill can be anything from digging a field latrine to firing a weapon.

The simple training methodology used to teach soldiers can be applied to train boys to be Adults and Citizens. Preparing for adulthood will not always be easy or fun. In fact, to achieve some of the skills will be challenging and take years. We Men will help our boys with their training. We want our boys to succeed and join the Brotherhood of Men. Remember what Heinlein said, "Don't handicap your children by making their lives too easy." Life is not always easy. You boys will face tests of strength and courage your entire adult life. You must prepare as a boy, to be a Man at 18. Of course, you still have to enjoy being a kid. Just not all the time. There is a ratio of hours working versus hours playing. There must be room for both over a Man's entire life. A Man must be able to experience joy in his life, and bring joy to others, to be complete.

Failing the test at 18 is very bad. I, as a member of society, would be looking for the Adults around him, the ones who failed the boy. All of us have a vested interest in seeing that every boy becomes a mature and responsible Adult, rather than the alternative. I would demand an explanation from those Adults and Elders responsible for this adulthood training.

So, what abilities must a boy possess to pass the Adult Manhood Test? Below is the "Skills Checklist — Adult." A boy must master the skills on the checklist to pass Manhood Test #1 — Adult, on his 18th birthday. All my skill checklists are a work in progress. If you think of a skill or two that should be added to the checklist, email me (gallantry@lanset.com). If you think I should delete a skill, or modify a skill, or if you have a better description and explanation of a skill, email me. My checklist may not be complete, but it's enough to get us started. If a boy trains hard, mastering each skill, he will pass the first test of Manhood, becoming a Man, and an Adult. We will conduct a special Rite-of Passage Manhood ceremony for the graduates. The reward for the newly recognized Men will be the Man Card. The privileges for Men holding a valid Man Card include talking to Women and driving a vehicle. No card, no woman, and no car. A male who flunks the test takes the bus until he gets his Man Card. Other privileges afforded Men possessing a valid Man Card are eating meat, using profanity, watching TV or videos, listening to music, and drinking alcohol. Males who fail don't get to enjoy a good burger, cursing, TV, music, or a cold beer. They are too busy studying to pass their Manhood Test to get the Card.

The new Man's loved ones, his friends, and all of America will call him a Man. The best part of "graduating" is that he will be welcomed as a member of the Brotherhood of Men.

If you are a male, already over 18, and flunk the Adult test, then you are wasting your life as a loser and you need to catch up. Reach out to the Men around you, and to your Elders, for help.
If you a boy under 18 reading this, then get off your lazy behind and get started. It's easy to start. Every day, starting right now, take a shower (adult skill 1), brush your teeth (adult skill 2), put on some decent looking, clean clothes (adult skill 3), and comb your

hair (adult skill 4). How simple is that? You will have successfully mastered the first four skills on the list in less than 30 minutes. Any average knucklehead can learn the first 10 basic skills. You're a really smart guy, you should have no trouble mastering all of them and passing the test.

Ready? Here we go!

SKILLS CHECKLIST — ADULT, 3rd Ed.

1. Bathing
2. Oral Care
3. Dressing
4. Grooming
5. Using a toilet
6. Eating/Feeding Yourself
7. Shopping
8. Cooking
9. General Cleaning and Chores
10. Laundry
11. Character Development
12. Organization
13. Punctuality
14. Health Management
15. Effective Interpersonal Communication
16. Etiquette, Manners
17. Proficient Student
18. Goal Setting
19. Citizenship
20. Driving
21. Courtship and Girls
22. Proper Use of Communication Methods
23. Managing Finances
24. Life/Career Planning
25. Pet/Animal Care
26. Work
27. Spirituality
28. Find A Place to Live
29. Quibbling
30. Stress and Anger Management
31. Property Management—Personal and Common Items

32. Borrowing and Loaning
33. Libido Management
34. Time Management
35. Teamwork
36. Good Decision Making
37. Followership and Leadership
38. Relationship Management
39. A Moral Compass
40. Don't Become a Professional Asshole

The first eight (8) skills are from a checklist—"Activities for Daily Living"—used by health care workers to determine if a person has sufficient physical and mental abilities to live on their own without adult supervision. When should a boy start training on a particular skill? Adulthood is the only manhood duty learned while still a child and adolescent. It will take about 15 years to get a boy ready for his first manhood test at 18. Skills 1 through 6, a boy should be able to master before he starts school. Skills 7 through 19, by the time he reaches the 7th grade. And the rest of the skills he masters while in high school.

I will list each adult skill and describe the breakdown of most of the major tasks within that skill, and if needed, a brief explanation of what "mastering" the skill looks like. Remember, if you read something that makes your eyebrows raise, or I did not explain clear enough, email me at gallantry@lanset.com.

ADULT SKILL #1 — BATHING

- A Man washes every day, using a clean wash rag, scrub brush,and lots of soap and hot water.
- He washes every square inch of his body except his eyeballs. Extra attention to the uniquely male bits, pieces, and crevices.
- He uses a clean towel to dry himself, not a dirty rag that's been on the floor for 6 months.
- A Man washes his hair with medicated shampoo to kill all the bugs—ticks, lice, fleas, spiders, crabs, maggots, etc.
- He wears fresh clean underwear and socks (if required) every day.

I added this first skill because when I was an Army Drill Sergeant training new young recruits, they were so filthy with their lack of basic hygiene that I had to conduct "hygiene inspection" every night for the first month, ensuring they showered, brushed, shaved, combed, and wore clean underwear and socks. They would have to hold up their dirty undies and socks so I could verify they were wearing clean skivvies. If I let them, some boys would wear the same underwear and socks over and over for months until the T-shirt turned yellow and the socks grew hard as rocks. My female Army Drill Sergeant colleagues tell me that their women basic trainees tend to be more hygienic than males. Females do seem to be more attracted to washing in hot soapy water than males are. A top complaint women have with males is their lack of basic hygiene.

> *"Some guys smell like ass.*
> *They seem quite comfortable going weeks, months even,*
> *without bathing or wearing clean clothing.*
> *I have no idea why boys love to be dirty and stinky all the time;*
> *like their rest rooms. " — Jackie S.*

ADULT SKILL #2 — ORAL CARE

- A Man brushes and flosses his teeth after every meal, or at least once per day before bedtime.
- He uses mouthwash and breath mints because he knows Women like their Men minty fresh and sparking clean.

ADULT SKILL #3 — DRESSING YOURSELF

- A Man is able to selected appropriate clothing for the situation. He is skilled with the different types of clothing worn for indoors, outdoors, school, church, etc.
- He can dress himself in clean, neat, well maintained clothes and shoes.
- A Man knows what to wear for a given function, like going to work or school.

I am not a fashionista. I know, as a man, that I must wear the correct clothing for the right occasion. For most events on my schedule, I can do it without help from my wife, Pat. For those special events, Pat cuts me some slack by picking out what to wear. She, not I, possesses the skill to select "outfits," matching top, pants, shoes, and accessories. One of the benefits of military service was that I always wore a uniform, something green, blue, or camouflaged. When I was off duty, it was T-shirts, shorts or levis, shoes or flip-flops. All clean, of course.

I believe with this adult skill, women understand and accept that most males have no color and outfit coordination abilities. Women generally are more skilled at shopping for clothes to make their men look nice. Pat told me that "If you wear what I buy, you will not look like a diaper-wearing Neanderthal." Her sister said, "I would be happy if a man can wear two clean socks of the same color."

ADULT SKILL #4 — GROOMING

- A Man properly grooms himself including: shaving, haircuts, combing hair, cleaning and trimming finger and toenails.
- He regularly cleans out the cheese in his ears, nose, and between his toes.
- A Man carries a clean handkerchief to blow his nose, never in public, in front of polite company, and/or women.

An exception. If a Man is not around women and is engaged in camping, hunting, or sports. No one would expect a Man to stop in the middle of the game to blow his nose on a clean hanky. Boys, keep your fingers out of your nose. Especially when you are around women and polite company.

- A Man does not spit unless he is a baseball player on the field or a cowboy at a rodeo. Or if he has pneumonia.

If you got a loogie the size of a golf ball in your throat, find a private place to spit it out. If you are at the head table of your sister's wedding, spitting on the dance floor would be disgusting.

"Most boys are slobs.
Most boys don't care how they look or smell." — Lee H.

ADULT SKILL #5 — USING A TOILET (indoors)

"I have never smelled anything more disgusting in my life,
than a boys' bathroom." – Anonymous Woman

I ask that you support my effort to demand that all bathrooms at home have a urinal. Most male toilet odor problems at home occur because of urination physics, the shape of the male anatomy, velocity of the flow, and the angle and distance to the water surface in your average toilet bowl. A fast flowing stream hitting the flat surface of water at high velocity makes for a mess. The problem is we men are being forced to use a plumbing device best suited to sitting down. In fact, my brother-in-law sits to pee. I would rather go out and pee with the dogs than sit to pee. That is just plain emasculating. Let me be the first to advocate a national referendum calling for installation of urinals in all home bathrooms.

As an Army Drill Sergeant, I had to personally supervise the Latrines (Army jargon for toilet), else the recruits would urinate and defecate everywhere.

Here are a few simple but important toilet tasks to master:

- "Brown" goes in the toilet, not on the floor, or in your pants.
- "Yellow" also goes in the bowl or urinal, not on the floor, walls,or in the hamper.
- ALWAYS flush when you finish. I do not care how much water you save by not flushing.
- Thoroughly wipe. Use a roll of toilet paper, wet wipes, and a pressure washer if you have to.
- Boys, wash those filthy hands—every time—before you exit the restroom.
- Seat up before you #1.
- Use lots of room freshener after you #2. You may think it smells like hot chocolate; others will not.

ADULT SKILL #6 — EATING/FEEDING YOURSELF, TABLE MANNERS.

"That boy is a P-I-G pig." — Babs, Movie, Animal House

This is another adult skill males have a problem mastering. While I find it difficult to actually eat like a pig, I have to admit when I was in the field (read: away from women), or in a Chinese all-you-can-possibly-eat buffet with the guys, my feeding habits required only a small shovel and a bucket.

When you have to be around women and polite folk, master the following:

- Men eat politely, with good table manners. Especially around company.
- A Man uses a knife, fork, spoon, and/or chopsticks to eat. Not your fingers unless it is a sandwich or fried chicken. I had a soldier in basic training who would eat everything with his bayonet. No fork or spoon, just a knife.
- A Man uses a napkin, not his sleeve or the tablecloth.
- He never chews his food with his mouth open or tries to stuff his face so full of food that he looks like a chipmunk storing nuts for the winter.
- A Man does not make animal noises while he chewing. Nor does he talk with his mouth full when he is around polite company and/or women.
- Man does not reach over others at the table for food. He asks others to pass the food to him.
- He does not take food off another person's plate unless he asks first and they say it's OK.
- A Man does not stuff himself until he can't breathe, unless he is with his "bros" at the Chinese buffet, and there are no polite company nor women present.

ADULT SKILL #7 — SHOPPING

- A Man must be able to shop for everything needed to live an adult life in the 21st century.
- Be able to make a shopping list, know where to buy the items,

and how to pay for them.
- Have an idea of how much things cost.
- Must learn how to do errands for self and others.
- A part of the shopping skill must include how to buy gifts, especially for the women in a Man's life, i.e. Mom, sister, wife, and girlfriend.

ADULT SKILL #8 — COOKING/MEAL PREPARATION

- A Man can buy fresh food and cook it.
- He can buy take out and heat up pre-made meals.
- He can read and follow recipes. Take some cooking classes.
- A Man can use a stove, oven, microwave oven, and basic kitchen equipment.
- He can set a table.
- He is able to menu plan, and prepare balanced nutritious dishes for breakfast, lunch, dinner, and snacks.

Master simple cooking:
- Roast meat on a BBQ—burgers, dogs, ribs, chicken.
- Cook potatoes, corn on the cob, and pasta.
- Make salads, big sandwiches, and use a deep fat flyer to make French fries.
- After each meal is prepared, a Man always cleans the kitchen (or BBQ), and does the dishes, etc.

ADULT SKILL #9 — HOUSEWORK/ CHORES/CLEANING

"Guys are the filthiest creatures on the planet.
I can't understand why they are so comfortable living in dirt!
A guy would not clean anything even if a giant germ
was holding his bathroom hostage!"
— Anonymous female observation

A boy in training should be:

- Doing chores as soon as he is out of diapers and old enough to walk; starting with putting away his toys; and tossing his clothes in a hamper.

- Keeping his living and sleeping area spotless by eight or nine years old.
- Capable of cleaning all rooms in the house, especially the bathroom and kitchen by 10 or 11 year old.
- Able to clean anything in the home by 12 or 13 years old—work/study area, garage, yards and garden, cars, dog, etc.
- Able to use the correct cleaning products and equipment for a specific cleaning job.

ADULT SKILL #10 — LAUNDRY

Too many moms are enabling their stay-at-home, adult-aged children by doing their laundry for them.

- A boy can wash and iron your own clothes by 12 years old.
- A Man can sort his own clothes; he knows how to use a washer, dryer, and iron.
- He knows which laundry products to use and how to apply them.
- Knows how to use dry cleaners.
- Women can teach boys how to launder female clothing properly so we don't screw it up.

ADULT SKILL #11 — CHARACTER DEVELOPMENT

This is a more advanced skill, requiring years of training, beginning when the boy is potty trained. Preschools are teaching character development to boys and girls as young as three years old.

"Character (defined) is the sum of the characteristics possessed by a person, especially to moral qualities, ethical standards, principles, and the like." (DEFINITION OF CHARACTER)

A male cannot be a Man without positive character traits. See a more comprehensive list of character traits in appendix 18. My list in the appendix is far from complete, however, it is a good start. There is a short list called the "Six Pillars of Character: Trustworthiness, Respect, Responsibility, Fairness, Caring, and Citizenship." (SIX) I would add four more to help Adults get ready to be husbands and fathers: patience, kindness, generosity, loyalty.

When a boy becomes a Man, he will be constantly judged by the content of his character. If he is a man of character, he will be respected. If he is a male with flawed character, he will be disrespected.

There are many excellent sources for character training. In my opinion, the best pre-military training is the Boy Scouts. A boy can start in the Cub Scouts at about seven years old. He can become a Boy Scout at about 11 or 12 years old until 18; or he can go on to the explorer program until about 23 years old. Scouts will teach a boy character as well as nearly everything he needs to be ready for the adulthood test. Unfortunately for the chronically lazy, the Scouts will make a boy do lots of ... what's that word? Oh, WORK.

ADULT SKILL #12 — ORGANIZATION

- A Man can manage all the parts of his life. He manages his daily routine and can deal with life's curve balls. A Man is in charge of his own life starting at 18 year old.
- Men are organized: keeping track of daily schedule like classes, work, appointments, dates, interviews, due dates for homework, bills, filing taxes, cashing in winning lottery tickets, etc. The simplest and cheapest way to master this task is to get a calendar/ appointment book. Read it every morning and read it before going to bed. Update it every day.
- Set up an "office" wherever you live, with a desk or table, chair, and some type of file cabinet or box for all your papers and files. Keep files for your receipts, legal documents like auto sales contracts, sales/repair agreements, car registration copies, insurance policies, warranties, leases, etc.
- You should carry with you, at all times, a pen and something to write on. I carry a small spiral notebook and a couple of free pens from businesses I visit. An easy way to carry paper is to take a blank 8 ½ x 11 sheet of printer paper, fold it up and put it in your wallet.
- Adults can read and understand basic legal documents including: simple contracts, insurance and medical forms,

sales documents, loan and credit contracts, leases and rental agreements, etc.

- A Man can use Microsoft Office or a similar suite.
- He can set up and use E-filing on his computer. Over 70% of my files are now electronic instead of paper. He also knows to back up his data.

I started carrying a pen and note book in the Army at 17. We were required to have them at all times. About 1999 I upgraded to a Palm Pilot for my daily schedule, for my "to do" list, and to keep memos, contact list, and voice memos. I hot sync my Palm with my desktop computer every day. The Palm is already obsolete technology, but still is reliable and old school. Those who want cutting edge get a Blackberry or other smart phone that can be synchronized with Microsoft Outlook.

ADULT SKILL #13 — PUNCTUALITY

- A Man gets there on time, a little early even. It is rude and disrespectful to be late for school, work, family events, appointments, classes, dates and meetings, etc. You could get fired for showing up to work late.
- Use that written schedule to keep yourself on time for your work schedule, classes, appointments, interviews, and for when stuff is due like homework, bills, and contracts, and for dates with your girlfriend, etc.
- Write all that stuff down.
- If you have a critical appointment, like a job interview, print out a map.
- Carry a time piece with you at all times. I used to say get a watch but most use the clocks on cell phones. Whatever, just get to where you've got to be on time or early.

On the rare occasion you do find yourself OBE (overcome by events)—and you know you will be late—call, if practical, to let them know that you will be late. Especially your doctor's office or your boss at work. Of course you would not call your professor who is teaching that class you are late for. But, you should apologize.

- Learn to land navigate. The Boy Scouts and the military do a great job of teaching map reading and land navigation. Get some maps of the area you live and travel around in. GPS systems are outstanding for getting to where you need to go. I used to carry about 50 maps in my vehicle until I got my first Global Positioning Satellite (GPS) navigation unit. Now I carry a few regional and state maps. I have used a GPS for 5 years in about 10 countries. I keep all the GPS maps updated and never travel without it.

ADULT SKILL #14 — HEALTH MANAGEMENT

A Man takes care of his health; his physical health, dental health, and mental health. There are three health care professionals a Man has in his address book: a primary care doctor, a dentist, and, when needed, a shrink. Yes, I included mental health. Americans, especially Men, tend to ignore their mental health due to ego and denial. We live in a modern, fast paced world that is anything but simple. Stress, anxiety, and depression are so common that most Americans have one or more of those maladies.

- Get an annual physical and dental exams.
- Get your teeth cleaned at least once a year. Twice or more if your month is particularly filthy.
- Sometimes you will have to take medication. Take your medications as prescribed. Learn how to refill your prescriptions and how to use over-the-counter medication like aspirin.
- Learn how to take care for yourself if you get a cold, or a headache, or are or hung over.
- GO TO THE DOCTOR OR EMERGENCY ROOM IF YOU GET REALLY SICK OR INJURED. An adult knows where the nearest ER is located and how to call for an ambulance.
- Adults are trained in First Aid, CPR, and how to use the new Automated External Defibrillators that are in most workplaces, schools, and some homes.
- A Man manages his health care insurance.

ADULT SKILL #15 — INTERPERSONAL COMMUNICATION

In academic terms, interpersonal communication is the process that we use to communicate our ideas, thoughts, and feelings to another person. It's all about sending and receiving messages with your fellow humans. A Man must be able to listen effectively, as well as speak properly and intelligently to individuals and small groups, whether communicating in person, electronically, or in writing. He must be understood and be able to understand those he is listening to.

- A Man is skilled at communicating on different interpersonal levels depending upon with whom he is conversing. For example, if a man is communicating with a family member, that communication will more than likely differ from the type of communication used when with a co-worker, or a significant other, or a child.

Be careful with your communication. It's too easy to have a big mouth. I have been blessed and cursed with a big mouth. I remember on one of my military efficiency reports, my boss wrote at the time that "Captain Lavelle rarely passed up the opportunity to make sure he was heard."

Being an effective (good) listener should be easy because a Man has two ears and one mouth so he can listen twice as much as he speaks. Right?

- Men learn and practice speaking and writing with proper grammar, vocabulary, and pronunciation. Nothing says "Ignorant Fool" faster than boy who speaks incoherently and writes illegibly.
- Men practice not saying anything too stupid. Learn to write neatly and literately.

ADULT SKILL #16 — ETIQUETTE and GOOD MANNERS

Etiquette means how you behave when in front of polite company.

- Men are courteous and respectful. Especially, in front of his parents, grandparents, teachers, and all other Elders.
- Men show respect to their elders by addressing them with the the honorific, "Sir," when talking to a male Elder, and "Ma'am" when addressing a female Elder.
- A Man shakes hands firmly and greets people properly.
- He does not use profanity in public unless he is a soldier on the battlefield or a ballplayer on the field. With other Men in private, cursing is acceptable. It is still discourteous in our culture to use profanity in the presence of women. Just because young women find it socially acceptable to curse like sailors, does not mean a Man should join in.
- A Man courteously greets everyone he meets or passes on the street with a "good morning," or "good afternoon," or some other simple, respectful acknowledgement of that other person's presence.
- A Man, always when passing another Man, makes brief eye contact, acknowledges that connection with a simple Man-to-Man greeting or a head nod of recognition. Long stares among males of most any mammal species are a threat and can be misinterpreted as a wish to engage in combat.

ADULT SKILL #17 — PROFICIENT STUDENT

- Men are excellent students.

They never take any training or education opportunity for granted. A man gets the right training and education for the goals he has set for himself. Men will always do their very best in training. They are polite and respectful students. They stay out of trouble. If a Man's goal is to go to college or learn a trade, then a Man knows how to prepare, how to enroll in college or in trade school, and knows what is required to graduate.

Do not go to college simply because you assume it is the only path to success. Too many boys fail in college because they attend without a crystal clear objective for why they are there. Any higher education plan, whether college or trade school, must end with the Man getting a well-paid job. A Man does not waste his time and money going to college until he has written in his life/

career plan his laser focused his education goal—that well-paying job. College is not necessary for everyone. A master electrician or plumber with a high school diploma can make well over $100K a year. If you do go to college, your ultimate goal is, I have said it twice already, that well-paid job. So, declare the right major.

Bob, the manager of our local Starbucks for the last 6 years, has a PhD in Philosophy from Stanford University. What was he thinking? Please do not Misunderstand me, philosophy is beneficial and still very relevant to our culture. I personally have studied and appreciate the discipline. With that said, what kind of high-paid job can a college degree in philosophy get? He can be a college teacher—that's it. I never saw any "battalion philosophers" in the military. I am not aware of corporate America hiring company philosophers. Bob admits, "I like to spout my opinion about the ways of the world. I picked that major because it was a degree in speaking BS. I never wanted to teach. I didn't think, at 18, about getting that really good job so I could start a family."

Studies show a trend that most Americans who do go to college major in liberal arts (history, art, philosophy, etc) rather than "hard science" like math, biology, or engineering. Two adults attend college. One majors in 17th century French poetry. The other majors in computer engineering and network design. Who will get the really good job? I never met a corporate poet in Silicon Valley.

ADULT SKILL #18 — GOAL SETTING

- Men set, for themselves, short, medium, and long-term goals.

Short-term goals are your new year's resolutions for the next year or so. Medium-term goals cover the next two to seven years. Long-term goals are over the next seven years through the rest of your life.

THE SINGLE MOST IMPORTANT GOAL FOR AN 18 YEAR OLD NEW ADULT IS WHAT HE IS GOING TO DO WITH THE FIRST TWO TO SEVEN YEARS OF HIS LIFE.

If you think of some goals, you have a 30% chance of achieving them. If you write your goals down and review them from time to time, you have an 80% chance of goal achievement. The trick with goal setting is to actually do them.

ADULT SKILL #19 — CITIZENSHIP

- A Man is also a loyal and involved citizen.

Adulthood and good citizenship are the first two of the four duties of a Man that start at 18. Chapter 4 discusses in more detail what a loyal and involved Citizen is, and what skills to master. Having said that, learning to be a good citizen starts when a male is still a young boy.

Citizen skills for a boy to master before reaching 18 years old:

- Obey the law.
- Be a good neighbor.
- Understand how government works.
- Know who their elected representatives are.
- Perform community service in some form.
- Learn about voter registration. Register at 18.

ADULT SKILL #20 — DRIVING/DRIVER'S LICENSE, TRANSPORTATION

A Man knows how to:

- Be a safe driver. Get a driver's license.
- Buy a car. Keep a car in good mechanical condition. Keep the car clean. Pay all car payments, insurance, and regular maintenance.
- Use any form of public transportation including: public buses, subways, light rail, taxi, etc.
- Travel by air or rail, including planning the travel, scheduling, and purchasing the tickets.
- Ride and take care of a bike.

ADULT SKILL #21 — GIRLS and COURTSHIP

This skill is so important, I will be writing a book specific to this subject: *The Courtship Manual—How to Woo Women and Find Good Wife.*

Courting is the process where a Man woos a woman. A Man is skilled at the art of "wooing" a woman, and in seeking her love, with intent of romance (and marriage).

- A Man is clear as to his courtship mission: to find the perfect woman to be his wife and mother of his children.
- A Man knows how to be polite and charming, making the women around him feel comfortable and secure.
- A Man can properly court and woo a woman. He knows how to approach and meet females, and how to make them feel happy, respected, and appreciated.
- A Man knows what qualities he wants in his Wife. Just like a woman should be crystal clear on what qualities she wants in a husband, and in the father of her children.
- A Man learns all he can about women: how they think; their behavior patterns; why they act the way they do; what is important to women; and what they want from men.

The fundamental steps of the human courtship ritual of western cultures, I'll use an example—for the continuity of my explanation of the courting process—a heterosexual human male and female, seeing each other for the first time, and becoming immediately smitten with that first eye contact. They fall deeply in love with each other, and then get married. Hey, stop laughing. It can happen!

COURTSHIP RITUAL STEPS

1. Selection for First Contact—the Man spots a potentially good woman
2. First Contact—first opportunity for the Man and Woman to meet and talk.
3. Subsequent Contact—not yet a date. Just informally meeting.
4. First Date—a planned get together to get to know each other

better.

5. Subsequent Dating—continuing the "getting to know you" connection process.
6. Mating—this may or may not happen depending on the values and ethnicity of the Man and woman.
7. Live Together—cohabitation, again, this may or may not happen depending on the values and ethnicity of the Man and woman.
8. Proposal—he asks her to marry him. She can say yes or no. If she says yes, then a wedding date is set.
9. Engagement—should be at least 2 years from the proposal date if couple has not been cohabiting, one year if they have.
10. Wedding—part ceremony, part party, should be a fun special day. The vows are the "oath" of the marriage.
11. Honeymoon
12. Marriage—the long haul of the relationship as defined in the marriage vows.
13. Children—yes or no? How many? Time line, when to start? Wait until resources in place (home, money, etc.).
14. Retirement—plan for 55 years old.

There is a relational attrition rate in each of the courtship steps. At any one of the steps, the relationship can end. Most end, for the Man at least, at step one (selection for first contact). He naturally will select a greater number of women than he will actually get to step two with. Human males and females non-verbally target each other for selection, deciding whether or not to make first contact. Usually in western cultures, males target females for selection and first contact. A man understands that few first contacts go on to a first date without step 3, subsequent contact. Fewer still going on to first date.

Sometimes the relationship makes it to marriage and children, only to end in divorce. At times, couples skip marriage and go straight to children. Or they don't have kids, but they live together for years without getting married.

Courting starts with step 1: selection, the period during which wooing takes place.

- A Man understands Homo Sapiens' mating biology and the rituals of human males and females. He understands his biological mating mission and hers.

In biology, "mating" is the pairing of the opposite sex for copulation, impregnation, and production and rearing of their offspring. Female humans are the only species on the planet that are "in heat" year round. Unlike primates, who mate seasonally within their troop a few times a year, we male humans can impregnate our females 365 days a year. The libidos of primate males "turn on and off" with the seasons. In human males, our libidos are "on" all the time. Therefore, the male human's biological mating mission is to dispense his genetic material into as many fertile human females as possible in his lifetime. With males, purely biologically speaking, it is all about the numbers. Males are physically capable of "dispensing" several times a day, to multiple females, every day of the year. The intense libido, the addictive craving that males have to mate with as many females as possible, can overwhelm an untrained and undisciplined male brain.

The female human's biological mating mission is all about offspring, to produce beautiful and healthy children. To accomplish her mission, she must, "cut from the herd," the biggest, handsomest, nicest, smartest, most loving and wealthiest male she can find, to impregnate her, and to be there as Husband and Father.

You "get it?" The seemingly conflicting gender mating biologies; guys want all the women, while girls want the one, the very best male. Women to have kiss a lot of toads to get find their prince, that one perfect Man. Females pick that one male almost by pure emotion. It's an emotional train wreck for them nearly every time because they pick badly most of the time.

The ritual mate selection process by females, the steps are something like this, as told to me by a wonderful lady named Jackie:

1. "The first is I meet this guy. He seems to be a keeper. He is big, strong, charming, and handsome. He makes me laugh and feel good. I'm thinking that I hope I don't fall in love with him too fast."
2. "Then I realize, oh shoot, too late, I love him."
3. "But wait, he is turning out to be a bastard who takes my money, cheats on me, and makes me cry a lot."
4. "No problem, I can fix him like Mom fixed Dad. We women have been training our men for decades."
5. "Oh, man, I give up. I really can't fix him."
6. "Now, my heart is broken and I have to leave him, the man I fell in love with. Damn!"
7. "Next, I go back to step 1 and repeat with the next guy I fall in love with. Once I get my heart broken a few more times, I will slip into my emotionally dark place, to become a jealous, unloved, man-hating, lesbian, psycho bitch!"

Girls, as part of their adult training, must be taught to pick the best Man logically, as well as emotionally. They must use both together to make a good selection of a Man. I designed a bonus test (chapter 5) just for this scenario. It helps a woman with her logical side.

> "Good judgment comes from experience,
> and a lot of that comes from bad judgment."
> — Will Rogers

ADULT SKILL #22 — USING COMMUNICATION DEVICES

- A Man can properly and courteously use just about all electronic communication methods and devices—telephones, internet, email, texting, smart phones, iPads, and, of course, social media. A man can communicate properly using any device he has mastered.

Before the Mesopotamians invented man's first writing system about 9,000 year ago, the only way man could communicate was by talking or signaling (i.e. drums, smoke, fire, etc.). There are so many ways for the 21st century American man to communicate.

- A Man is expected to be literate—able to speak, read, and write English with enough skill that he is understood and he can understand others who speak English. It can be in any language. But, in several countries (India, Pakistan, Philippines, etc.), the people speak so many different languages that they use English as the language of Government, Business, and Education. Americans should adopt that policy in America.
- A Man uses good manners while communicating, and is courteous and respectful.
- He knows how to type on all keyboards that he uses.
- A Man is respectful of others by not disturbing them while using a communication device.
- He realized that there is no privacy in cyberspace. He is careful what he "puts out there."
- A Man embraces new technology. He can obtain a cell phone, high speed internet, a computer, and email, and he can text.

ADULT SKILL #23 — MANAGING FINANCES

- A Man knows how to make some money.
- He can manage his money.
- He has a financial plan.

A Man must, unsupervised, be able to:

- Open, utilize, and manage a bank savings account, a checking account, an ATM and Debit card.
- Apply for and properly manage a low interest credit card. Payoff the entire balance every month. Rarely carry over a balance, paying interest.
- Balance and reconcile all bank accounts monthly.
- Start and manage an investment/retirement account: interest drawing savings, IRA, life insurance, etc.
- Master basic accounting software to manage his personal finances.
- Prepare and file federal and state tax returns. He can complete IRS W-4 Forms (withholding).
- Complete and submit scholarship and student loan paperwork.
- Understands basic economics, such as stock markets, Federal Reserve, GDP, inflation, marketplace, deficit spending, etc.

- Maintains good credit and FICO score.
- Maintains proper cash flow, pays all his bills on time.

To help their boy master this skill, parents should establish a lump sum, allowance system as soon as the boy can count, do simple math, and understand the concept of money. Email me if you want a copy of the system, gallantry@lanset.com.

ADULT SKILL #24 — PET/ANIMAL OWNERSHIP AND CARE

- A Man takes care of all animals he is responsible for, every day. The basics include: feeding, grooming, and cleaning any kennels or cages, vet medical care as required, training and playtime.
- A man can assess types of pets, and how many he can responsibly manage.
- A man enjoys all the animals in his care.

If a Man travels a lot, then maybe no pets. If a man works 60 hours a week locally, he probably should not get a high energy hunting dog. A couple of cats may be better. On the other hand, a retired police or military working dog is a good idea for the busy working man. They sleep most of the day and night and require little exercise.

A boy can't take care of himself, let alone another living creature. If a boy has to have a pet, get him a plastic plant, a sandwich, or some dead insects. Only when a boy demonstrates enough maturity and responsibility can he have a pet. I recommend a cat since cats are lower maintenance. If he does well with the cat, then maybe get a dog next. Having a pet is good practice for being a Father. Stick with dogs and cats. Skip reptiles and small mammals as pets.

I am proud to be an American. But, I am deeply embarrassed by how irresponsible our society with our pets. We throw our puppies and kittens out with the garbage. In my county (Sacramento), the Pound and ASPCA kill thousands of unwanted dogs and cats every year. It's an embarrassment that taints the pride I have in my great nation. I suggest we change getting a dog license for the dog. Instead, a dog license should be for the human who wants to own a dog. It would be proof that he has acquired the training and resources to care for a dog. Just my 2 cents on this subject.

ADULT SKILL #25 — WORK/FIND A JOB

- A Man has a work ethic.

I mentioned at the beginning of the book, The Protestant Work Ethic: "A view of life that promotes hard work and self-discipline as a means to material prosperity. It is called Protestant because some Protestant groups believe that such prosperity is a sign of God's grace." (PROTESTANT)

A boy starts mastering this skill as soon as he can walk. In Adult Skill #9, I said a boy's first "job" is usually "put away your toys." Followed by, "clean up your room." The layering of more complex and more frequent work around the house starts the work ethic imprinting. If a boy starts young, it will be easier to add more strenuous and more complicated work tasks as he gets closer to 18.

- A Man can always find employment, a paying job. I say again, a Man can always find a paying job. Even if he has a PhD in philosophy. Starbucks is always hiring.
- A Man can find the right job, the type of work in an environment that pays well, and one that he enjoys. A Man works more efficiently if he enjoys his job and is paid well enough to live in a style he is most comfortable with. For most Americans, that is the middle-class.
- A Man figures out what job he wants, he networks, he gets trained for it, then he applies, interviews, and gets hired.
- A Man knows how to keep a job. He is a reliable worker.
- A Man works his entire life until retirement, unless he makes his fortune, enough to retire immediately.

Mastering this skill takes time. You have to start imprinting the work ethic while they are very young, so they are conditioned to work and will not complain or resist as much. A boy should be performing chores to develop his work ethic and earn his allowance. By about 14 to 16 years old, the boy should be working part time at a local business.

ADULT SKILL #26 — FIND A PLACE TO LIVE

A Man must:

- Calculate his cost of living budget, setting up a living arrangement, alone or with roommates.
- Be able to locate suitable housing on or under his budget.
- Complete all lease/rental agreements.
- Obtain and maintain renters insurance.
- Keep the housing clean and in good order.
- Obtain utilities to include internet, cable/satellite TV, gas, electric, etc.
- Maintain a professional relationship with his landlord and neighbors.
- When budget allows, be able to buy housing.

When a boy turns 18, still living at his parents' home, he should pay rent for his room, meals, internet and cell service, his share of the cable and utilities, etc. He has to learn that having a warm and safe roof over one's head and enjoying some creature comforts is not free. Somebody is paying for it. Usually Mom and Dad.

ADULT SKILL #27 — LIFE/CAREER PLANNING

- A Man always has a life/career plan penciled out, outlining his short, medium, and long term life goals. When he turns 18 and passes Manhood Test #1 — Adult, he will be expected to execute that plan.

Boys, waiting until you are 18 to figure out what you want to do with your life is too late.

This is a skill you must have mastered before you're 18. By 16 years old, you must start thinking about what you are going to do with your first 4 to 7 years of adult life. Think of how you see yourself as a Man living on your own after high school. What will that look like? Unfortunately, many young males drift aimlessly well into their twenties, early thirties even, before they finally figure it out. Others never think it through and wind up on the streets, on drugs, or in jail.

To you newly minted Men, I say you are done with high school. You are now 18 years old. You passed the Adult Manhood Test. You are counting the days to getting out of the house and living on your own. If you had some plan in place, you would be making your move to courageously live in society as a Man and an Adult. Regrettably, we have made life at home too comfortable. I believe most young adult males are clueless about the world, maybe even afraid to venture out in it.

Here is a little list to help the boys work their plan. There are about 6 options after high school.

Ask yourself, "Do I want to:

1. Be a couch potato, sitting around my parent's house all day, smoking dope and playing video games?
2. Go to college, and graduate with a degree in a field that leads to a well-paid job I will enjoy?
3. Join the military or Peace Corps for personal growth and a little fun, travel, and adventure? And pick up over $60K in college scholarship money.
4. Enroll in a vocational trade school to learn to service or build computers, or undergo training in welding, electrician, or truck driving?   Anything you would enjoy doing and make good money at it.
5. Stay at Starbucks forever, where I have been working since I was a junior in high school?
6. Do a mix of this list over the next 2 to 7 years?"

Do you want to be a firefighter, billionaire businessman, or scientist, or an artist, carpenter, or pilot? Do you want to invent to cure for cancer, work on your own farm, or travel the world as a soldier, explorer, diplomat, or college professor?

It really doesn't matter what you do so long as you can live respectably, support yourself, and when he time comes, your wife and children. Start by writing down your goals for the first 4 to 7 years of your adulthood. What do you want to do, where do you want to live, how will you make money, etc. Your plan needs to stay flexible, so write it out in pencil. Keep it on your desk to update it as your life progresses and new opportunities and roadblocks pop up. Plan in pencil.

If anyone out there wants some life/career plan ideas and sample plans, email me, gallantry@lanset.com.

ADULT SKILL #28 — SPIRITUALITY

- A Man has some brand of spirituality in him. To master this skill, a Man must fill the faith spot in his brain with something.

Scientists have found a spiritual side to our species, a part of the brain called, "The God Spot." Researchers say they have located the parts of the brain that controls religious faith. The research proves, they contend, that belief in a higher power is an evolutionary asset that helps human survival. The researchers said their findings support the idea that the brain has evolved to be sensitive to any form of belief that improves the chances of survival. (CONNER)

I believe a Man will miss finding joy in his life if his "God Spot" is empty. The cool thing about spirituality is a Man can fill his spot with whatever works for him: religion, atheism, secular theology (systematic study of the existence or nonexistence and nature of the divine and its relationship to and influence upon other beings). What he "fills his spot" with can be anything from joining big or small religions, yoga, meditation, or martial arts.

Humanism could fill your spot if that's what works for you. Humanism is a philosophy that focuses on human values and concerns, attaching prime importance to human rather than divine or supernatural matters. You can just sit at a beautiful spot by the river and fish if that fills your spot. Fishing has the tranquility of Zen. It is not just about catching fish.

Do not leave your spiritual center empty. Find something that fills your spirituality or I believe you will not find joy in your life. Worse, you will not bring any joy to others.

I was born and raised a Roman Catholic. I stopped practicing about my first tour in Vietnam and never looked back. As I have grown older, I found myself missing something. I got into my own blend of a bit of Daoism, with touch of Zen, Hinduism, and a dash of Saganism.

The astronomer Carl Sagan said, "Some people think God is an outsized, light-skinned male with a long white beard, sitting on a throne somewhere up there in the sky, busily tallying the fall of every sparrow. Others—for example Baruch Spinoza and Albert Einstein—considered God to be essentially the sum total of the physical laws which describe the universe. I do not know of any compelling evidence for anthropomorphic patriarchs controlling human destiny from some hidden celestial vantage point, but it would be madness to deny the existence of physical laws." (SAGAN)

I believe there exists in the universe what I would call "The Great Mystery."

ADULT SKILL #29 — QUIBBLING

Quibbling is "back talking" or getting whiny and defensive when an adult is giving a male feedback on some bad behavior. Quibbling includes whining, complaining, sniveling, blubbering, etc. Boys whine like a two year old with a load in his diaper.

- Men don't whine or quibble. Period. They maintain a "can do" attitude" and value feedback from their friends and family so they can grow and learn from it rather than getting defensive.
- Men don't make excuses for their failures. They accept that they are flawed like we all are, and they will learn to do better.

ADULT SKILL #30 — STRESS and ANGER MANAGEMENT

• A Man must be able to stay cool and calm when it hits the fan. That is, "...any circumstance or event that's inadvertently or intentionally complicated or compounded by stupidity, arrogance, incompetence, or inefficiency, with potentially disastrous results is more politely known as the "defecation hit the oscillation." It is a truism of such rotational dispersion that whatever good or bad hits the fan will NOT be evenly distributed!" (MIL TERMS S-SIERRA) When it hits the fan, there must be somebody with a clear head who can keep his composure and calmly handle the "event."

Most boys get furious, out-of-control angry, over the most insignificant of inconveniences. I have personally seen college aged males in such a state of rage that they put their heads through walls, destroy car windows, rip down window and doors, and throw televisions out the window.

• A Man learns how to control his anger so he will not get out of control and do something stupid he will later regret.
• A Man, especially a Father, must be patient and bring calm to his family—not add stress.

However, staying cool and calm has its price on a Man's psyche. Anger needs a non-abusive outlet to release stress and emotion, else it may, over time, affect his physical and mental health. He can try boxing or karate, a tremendous stress reliever. You get to kick, punch, and hit other guys in a controlled environment. For something less violent, consider yoga or swimming, even the very mellow Tai Chi. In Tai Chi, one learns to relax by meditation, an outstanding tension reducer.

There was a wrecking yard around here where, for a $10.00 donation to a veteran's organization, they let you use sledge hammers to beat on any vehicle in the yard, for as long as you can swing the hammer. What a great tactic to lower anxiety.

ADULT SKILL #31 — BORROWING and LOANING

- A Man can borrow another person's property, and return it on time in the same condition (or better) than he got it. If he loses or damages it he will apologize and immediately offer to pay for a replacement or repair.

When I was still in the Army, I attended a drinking party in the barracks. I accidently threw another soldier's three year old 21" Color TV into the street. The next day I bought, delivered, and set up a new 27" TV for my comrade. All was forgiven. My punishment was money from my pocket for a new TV. One of the privileges of being a Man is that he is authorized to drink adult beverages. In addition, he may occasionally get intoxicated. Breaking a buddy's TV is something a man can recover from if he takes care of it fast.

> "Whatever happens, take responsibility."
> — Tony Robbins

- A Man will loan his property only to other Men. Period. He will not loan his property to a boy unless an Adult can supervise.
- A Man does not loan money unless he is clear on the terms, payment due dates and amount. Or he makes it clear to the borrower that he intends to give that money away as a gift with no expectation of payback.

ADULT SKILL #32 — PROPERTY MANAGEMENT

- Men respect and take care of their personal property (from clothes, to a car, or a house) and the property of others they are responsible for.
- He will keep track of all property he is accountable for, and keep it in good working order, replacing it as needed.
- He will try to minimize hoarding and pack ratting.

ADULT SKILL #33 — LIBIDO MANAGEMENT

From an anthropologist point of view, "A yawning chasm separates the reproductive life of human females from that of the females of the other three million sexually reproducing species.

We are the only female species capable of sexual union year-around rather than only when they are 'in heat.' Homo sapiens are the only species with a brain that is capable of overriding the circuitry that demands obedience to our sexual urges, allowing us to refrain from sexuality for the purpose of choosing when and if we become pregnant, and also allows us to be highly selective in our choice of a mate." (EDEN)

The conflict over sex and mating is caused by opposing human reproductive biology. A male Homo sapiens' reproductive mission is to copulate with as many females as possible in his lifetime. Human males assess all human females he can see as potential mating partners. Every human female can count on a large group of males ready and willing to mate with her. She needs that array of males because her biological reproductive mission is to choose the one perfect male specimen from the herd to be her Husband and Father of her children. It seems so "Darwinian" when you think about it. Males want all females. Females want the one best male. We assume she will pick the "finest" male from the group of males who want to mate with her. More on that myth later.

The science is clear. Boys, you must get a grip on your libido. The old saying goes, "use the big head to do the thinking." Males are out of control when it comes to sex.

- A Man manages his libido.
- He practices certain techniques that enable him to keep his libido under control.

In my book, *The Courtship Training Manual—How to Woo Women and Find a Good Wife,* I will discuss a libido management technique I developed to enable a man to communicate with a woman without her feeling like a piece of meat. I call it the "Positive Male Experience," or "PME" technique. Before the PME technique was perfected and taught to males, the mission of the male human making a first contact with a female human was to assess her willingness to immediately mate with him. That's about all the justification an untrained young male needs for a reason to approach a female.

The PME technique is a totally different approach to first contact and subsequent contact in social interpersonal communications with females. The PME technique in communicating with a female focuses the males attention on developing an emotional link, making the female feel at ease and comfortable with him. PME will put her in a good mood, put a smile on her face, maybe even to get her to laugh. That's it. No male libido agenda is at work. He's just making an interpersonal connection to bring a little joy to her life, and the Man wants to find joy for himself in that moment they share together.

When a Man, using the PME technique, makes subsequent contact with that same women, eventually she feels more relaxed and safe around a Man because she trusts him to treat her respectfully. Making a woman laugh and putting a smile on her face is the basic process of being charming. If she sees that same guy again, she will already be smiling because she will remember how charming he was.

I have field tested the PME technique. It works. The Man can relax because he is not "on the hunt." The Woman can relax because she feels safe and comfortable, enjoying the Man's honest charm and humor.

ADULT SKILL #34 — TIME MANAGEMENT

This skill is related to the organization and punctuality skills. Time management is the act or process of planning and exercising conscious control over the amount of time spent on specific activities, especially to increase efficiency or productivity.

- A Man organizes his time so he can get done what needs doing, and maybe have some spare time to find a little joy in his life.
- Men use their written schedule and some type of clock to track their time; men do not miss appointments and events where they have to be at a certain time. All smart phones contain appointment management programs. Use it.

ADULT SKILL #35 — TEAMWORK

- Men are loyal team members and competent team leaders.
- A Man joins some type of team: sports, scouts, recreation, military, school, work, etc.
- He puts the needs of his teammates before his own needs.
- A Man is "mission focused."

Being a member of a team teaches a boy to put the needs of others before his own. He learns to care more about the team than himself. He trusts his teammates to "have his back," knowing they will pick him up him if he falls, as he would do the same for his teammates. Why would a soldier, without a moment's hesitation, jump on a live grenade, killing himself instantly, saving his buddies? Why would he do that? Because his actions represent how far a Man is willing to go to protect his teammates. It is not unusual for wounded soldiers to sneak out of the hospital and return to their unit. Even though they could go home, they would rather be with their team. A Man's bond to his team is so strong that it is more important to him not to let the team down than it is to protect his own physical health. How often do professional athletes continue to play the game even though they are injured?

Another important part of teamwork is "mission focus." Keeping his eye on the ball, whether it is to win the game, build the bridge, or fight the battle, a man holds nothing back in doing his part to accomplish the team's mission.

ADULT SKILL #36 — GOOD DECISION MAKING

- A Man makes good decisions ... most of the time. He arrives at the best decisions he can, within the time limit, using the information he has available to him at the moment he has to make that decision.
- A Man has good judgment and common sense; that ability to make a decision objectively, authoritatively, and wisely, especially in serious or consequential matters.
- A Man rarely fails to make a decision—good or bad.

"I would rather follow a commander
whose decisions may not be right all the time,
than an incompetent leader
who can make no decisions at all."
— Anonymous Army Sergeant.

We make so many decisions every day, big and small, from what to order off the menu, to what to watch on TV, to proposing to the right girl, to sending men to the moon or into combat. I have heard of a study floating around that examined the rates of good decision making by age. A 14 year old boy makes about 40% correct decisions every day. A trained and experienced decision maker, like a military sergeant or general, or a police officer, makes about 85% correct decisions. No one is 100%. No one is even 90% correct, everyday of his life.

- A Man practices making good decisions under various situations and time constraints.

How serious is the decision he will have to make? How much time does he have to make it? How much information does he have at his disposal to assist him in making the best decision he can?

There are a couple of types of human decision makers: those who need lots of time and lots of information before they can make a decision, and those who need little time and not much information to make that same decision. One could assume that with more time and information, one would have a better chance to make the correct decision. I am not so sure more time and information is always needed to make correct decisions. I have a friend in the "more time and information" group. He can stare at a menu for over 30 minutes, unable to decide what to order. I have seen him take 10 minutes to order at McDonald's. He drives me crazy. Being a soldier most of my life, I make most decisions quickly. The difficult take longer, but in the end I make a decision.

Boys, the 40% good decision adolescents with undeveloped brains, make some reckless and negligent decisions that result in ambulances, fire trucks, and police. Movies and TV glamorize knuckleheads doing reckless jackass stunts. Boys with underdeveloped brains don't think about the consequences or who their decision will hurt.

A good strategy to assist young decision makers to stay out of trouble is to take a little time to get more information, to weigh the options.

He can ask himself if his decision will:

1. Get me, or anyone else killed or wounded?
2. Damage and/or destroy my property, or the property of others?
3. Get me or anyone else arrested and/or put in jail or prison?
4. Cause disrespect and/or embarrassment to myself, my friends, family, co-workers, etc?
5. Get me, or any else, sued?

ADULT SKILL #37 — RELATIONSHIP MANAGEMENT

- A Man considers all of his relationships to be important and worthy of his time.
- A Man cultivates and maintains his relationships. His philosophy is to give more of himself and to expect less from others in maintaining and managing healthy relationships.
- He stays in touch.

An interpersonal relationship is an association between two or more people that may range from fleeting to enduring. This association may be based on, love, solidarity, regular business interactions, or some other type of social commitment. Interpersonal relationships are formed in the context of social, cultural and other influences. The context can vary from family or kinship relations, friendship, marriage, relations with associates, work, clubs, neighborhoods, and places of worship. They may be regulated by laws, customs, or mutual agreements; they are the basis of social groups and society as a whole. A relationship is normally viewed as a connection between two individuals, such as a romantic or intimate relationship, or a parent-child relationship. Individuals can also have relationships with groups of people, such as the relation between a pastor and his congregation, an uncle and a family, or a mayor and a town. Interpersonal relationships usually involve some level of interdependence. People in a relationship tend to influence each other, share their thoughts and feelings, and engage in activities together. Because of this interdependence, most things that change or impact one member of the relationship will have some level of impact on the other member. (BERSCHEID)

Relationships, personal and professional (work), must be nurtured and cared for. "Relational currency" is the concept of keeping a relationship up to date and fresh. A Man must get along respectfully with other humans. He learns that each relationship is unique and must be "kept current" if it is to survive and endure, especially with a Man's family, friends, co-workers, neighbors, roommates, etc.

I tend to reach out, to give, more than others. It's more important to me to keep the relationship current than to point fingers, saying, "Why don't you ever call me!"

Stay in touch with those who want to hear from you, like your mom. Learn about non-verbal communication, especially to help you better understand women.

ADULT SKILL #38 — A MORAL COMPASS

- A Man has a moral compass.
- He clearly knows the difference between right and wrong, good and bad.

Morals are the principles or rules of right conduct or the distinction between right and wrong. A compass shows us the direction to go. Therefore, a "moral compass" is anything, a value or character trait maybe, that serves to direct or guide a Man's decisions based on morals.

A moral compass shows us if the direction is "Good," "Bad," or in what is called "The Gray Area." Men know the difference between right and wrong. They learn it from family, religion, society, military, scouts, etc.

ADULT SKILL #39 — LEADERSHIP and FOLLOWERSHIP

- A Man is an effective and competent leader, who can build a lead a cohesive team.
- He is a loyal "follower," and team member, who can be counted on do his part to accomplish the team's mission.
- A Man is never a "control freak" or an incompetent leader because he practices "responsibility of control."

"Lead, follow, or get out of the way."
— Thomas Paine, American Writer

"You manage things; you lead people."
— Grace Murray Hopper, American Computer Programmer

A boy is taught leadership and followership in incremental steps. First, he learns to be a good follower, a team member. Then, he steps into small leadership roles, leading to larger and larger leadership responsibilities as he matures. A boy learns the different styles of leadership, and learns which style to use with each individual follower/teammate. He learns about his own limitations that will affect his ability to lead.

Most importantly, a boy masters responsibility of control. He understands that the male gender is in control of nearly everything in our world from governments and corporations, to the family and community. He knows that control is power. As the quote says:

"With great power there must also come — great responsibility!"
— Stan Lee, American Writer

- Men respect the power of being in control. They strive to use it for good, not evil.

This skill overlaps some with the Adult skill #35 — Teamwork. A good leader can build a cohesive team that will always keep their eye on the ball. The "ball" is the mission. Earlier I said that men run everything in the world. We are in charge of governments, corporations, the military, etc. A Man is a team player who learns to put the needs of the team first. A boy must learn leadership and followership on his path to adulthood. Play on a sports team, join high school or college ROTC, or the Boy Scouts.

ADULT SKILL #40 — DON'T BECOME A PROFESSIONAL ASSHOLE

* A Man is, at no time, a "Professional Asshole."

He is, on rare occasion when he must be, an amateur asshole until what needs doing is done. Then he "reverts" to his normal courteous, kind, and caring demeanor. A good analogy is the differences between Bruce Banner and The Hulk. Bruce is a mild mannered nice guy. But when Banner gets angry and stressed out, he turns into The Hulk, a big green scary angry monster who can rip people in half and throw buses through buildings. When The Hulk clams down, he reverts back to the mellow Banner.

Humans are very judgmental. We tend to label others quickly. You boys will notice that as you work your way to Manhood, people will start calling you a Man. However, as you are handing your business as you should be, they may also start calling you an asshole. Men who take care of their responsibilities as men, tend to be labeled as an asshole from time to time.

There are two types of assholes—"professional" and "amateur." A "Professional Asshole" makes a living as a full time asshole. To them it's a lifestyle and career choice. They have their own websites and magazines. Those jerks firmly believe that a professional asshole is an accomplishment that few life forms can achieve. They find it something to be proud of; they believe that not all men are cut out to be as much of an asshole as they are. A professional asshole is a male known by many names: "evil, narcissistic, ignorant, bully, creep, jerk, tyrant, tormentor, despot, back stabber, egomaniac, flat out rude, nasty, selfish, oppressive, uncivil, mean-spirited, and really don't seem to care about whom they step on." (SUTTON)

There are not that many professional assholes around, thank

God. It takes a lot of work to be a professional asshole. The more benign type is the "amateur asshole." We Men, if we are out there handling our business, will get called asshole from time to time, mostly because among judgmental people the threshold to reach the level of "assholeness" to the point of being called an asshole is fairly low. Remember, most of us Men are the more benign, amateur type of asshole. As I said before, think of an amateur asshole as being The Hulk. If The Hulk is the asshole, then Bruce Banner is the normal mild-mannered guy. We only see The Hulk when Banner is really pissed off and needs to kick some ass. Once that is done, The Hulk reverts back to Banner. Get it?

As I was researching this topic for the book I found that the simple definition of asshole is "A person who is irritating." I thought to be an asshole, a man had to have all the traits of a professional. Now I find out I just have to irritate somebody and I am automatically labeled an asshole. Fortunately, now that we can distinguish the two types of asshole, most Men fall into the "Amateur Asshole" category. I say to my fellow Men out there getting it done, be proud of being called an asshole once in awhile by your family (especially your kids), co-workers, and teammates. It means you are indeed getting done what a Man needs to get done. Men should no longer have to be embarrassed nor feel disrespected when appropriately being called an asshole.

MANHOOD TEST #1 — ADULT, 5th Ed.

If you have any suggestions to make this and any other test a more effective tool, please email me personally, gallantry@lanset.com.

Once all the training is completed, the last step to adulthood is to administer the first test of manhood: Manhood Test #1 — Adult. Pass the test and a boy is an adult and a man. Fail and he remains a boy in remedial training until he can be tested again.

The test is administered by a minimum of three adults, who have intimate knowledge of the boy's training and preparation for adulthood. Test administrators should include a combination of parents, teachers, clergy, or Elders. The boy being assessed should be present in case a test administrator wishes to ask the boy any questions.

Administer this test periodically before the boy turns 18 to determine what his weak areas are for further training. The official test is taken between 17 ½ and 18 ½ years old. If he fails at 18 ½, he must participate in remedial training. A boy can be tested repeatedly until he can pass the examination. Once he has been deemed ready to take the test again, the entire examination will be repeated.

DIRECTIONS TO TEST ADMINISTRATOR:
1. Read all 40 questions.
2. Score each question 0 to 10 points.
3. Total the score (400 points maximum).
4. Use the scoring chart at the end of the test to determine pass or fail and the status of the tested boy.

SCORING TIPS: You can score each question from zero (0) to a maximum of ten (10) points. When evaluating the question, consider whether the male you are testing has 100% succeeded on a particular question; that's 10 points. If he is near perfect, then that is an 8 or 9. If the guy is missing a important part of the skill, that is a 3 to a 7. If he is nearly failing, that is 1 or 2 points. And finally, if this guy you're testing is clueless on a skill, or just totally failing, that is ZERO points. Your subjectivity comes into play. The bottom line is your scoring will determine if this guys is an Adult and a Man ... or not. Be hard, be ruthless in your scoring. We cannot allow any male who is not ready to slip through.

Consider mastering the Adult skills and passing the first Manhood Test as a rite-of-passage. If you pass a boy, and he fails to perform as an adult, you may have to explain why you passed him. Remember the Heinlein quote, "Never handicap your children by making their lives too easy." This test must take years to prepare for and be tough to pass. Remember, no matter how hard we train and mentor and prepare our boys for the test, some guys were just never meant to be adults. A certain percentage will be chronic failures for a variety of reasons.

40 multipart questions. 10 points each.
400 points total.

1. BATHING. Does he wash every day, using a clean wash rag, a scrub brush, and lots of soap and hot water? Does he use a clean towel to dry, not a dirty rag that's been on the floor for 6 months? He washes his hair with shampoo? Does he wear fresh clean underwear and socks every day?

2. ORAL CARE. Does he brush and floss teeth daily after every meal, or at least once per day before bedtime? Does he use mouthwash and breath mints?

3. DRESSING YOURSELF. Is he able to select appropriate clothing for the situation? Is he able to dress himself in clean, neat, well-maintained clothes and shoes? Does he know what to wear for a given function, like going to work or school?

4. GROOMING. Does he regularly shave, get a haircut, comb his hair, clean and trim his fingernails and toenails? Does he carry a clean handkerchief to blow his nose? Does he keep his fingers out of his nose? Does he spit in public?

5. USING A TOILET. Does he put the "brown" in the toilet, not on the floor or in his pants? Does he put the "yellow" in the bowl or urinal, not on the floor, walls, or in the hamper? Does he ALWAYS flush when finished? Does he thoroughly wipe? Does he wash his hands every time after using the toilet?

6. EATING/FEEDING/TABLE MANNERS. Does he eat politely, with good table manners? Does he use a knife, fork, spoon, or chopsticks to eat, and not his fingers, unless it is a sandwich or fried chicken? Does he use a napkin, not his sleeve or table cloth? Does he chew his food with his mouth open, or stuff his face with so much food he looks like a chipmunk storing nuts for the winter? Does he make animal noises while he chews? Does he talk with food in his mouth? Does he reach over others at the table for food? Does he take food away from others without asking permission? Does he stuff himself until he can't breathe?

7. SHOPPING. Is he able to shop for everything needed to live an Adult life in the 21st century? Can he make a shopping list, know where to buy the items, and how to pay for them? Does he know what things cost and how to shop for the best value? Does he do errands for himself and others? Does he buy gifts,

especially for the women in his life: his mom, sister, wife, and girlfriend?

8. COOKING/MEAL PREPARATION. Can he buy food? Can he cook fresh food as well as heat up pre-made meals? Can he read and follow recipes? Can he use a stove, oven, microwave oven, and basic kitchen equipment? Can he set a table? Is he able to menu plan and prepare balanced nutritious dishes for breakfast, lunch, dinner, and snacks? After each meal is prepared, does he clean the kitchen (or BBQ) and do the dishes, etc?

9. HOUSEWORK/CHORES/CLEANING. Does he do chores? Does he keep his living and sleeping area spotless? Does he clean all rooms in the house, especially the bathroom and kitchen? Can he clean anything in the home: work/study area, garage, yards and garden, cars, dog, etc? Does he know how to use the correct cleaning products and equipment for a specific cleaning job?

10. LAUNDRY. Does he wash and iron his own clothes? Does he sort his own clothes? Does he know how to use a washer, dryer, and iron? Does he know which laundry products to use and when? Can he use a dry cleaners?

11. CHARACTER DEVELOPMENT. Does he possess the positive character traits of: trustworthiness, respect, responsibility, fairness, caring, citizenship, patience, kindness, generosity, and loyalty?

12. ORGANIZATION. Does he manage all the parts of his life? Is he organized; does he keep track of his daily schedule, like classes, work, appointments, dates, interviews, due dates for homework, bills, filing taxes, cashing in winning lottery tickets, etc? Does he possess a calendar/appointment book? Does he read and update it every morning or before going to bed? Does he keep files for his receipts and legal documents like auto sales contracts, sales/repair agreements, car registration copies, insurance policies, warranties, leases, etc? Does he, at all times, carry a pen and something to write on? Can he read and understand basic legal documents, including: simple contracts, insurance and medical forms, sales documents, loan and credit contracts, leases and rental agreements, etc?

13. PUNCTUALITY. Does he get there on time, a little early even? Does he use that written schedule to be on time for work,

classes, appointments, interviews, etc? Is he on time for when stuff like homework and bills are due and for dates with a girlfriend, etc? Does he carry a time piece at all times? Does he, on the rare occasion when he will be late, call to let them know he will be late? Can he use a map and/or GPS?

14. HEALTH MANAGEMENT. Does he take care of his health: his physical health, dental health, and mental health? Does he get an annual physical and dental exam? Does he get his teeth cleaned at least once a year? If required, does he take his medication as prescribed? Can he refill his prescriptions? Does he know how to use over-the-counter medication like aspirin? Can he care for himself if he gets a cold, headache, or is hung over? Is he trained in First Aid, CPR, and how to use the newest Automated External Defibrillators that are in most workplaces, schools, and some homes? Does he manage his health care insurance?

15. INTERPERSONAL COMMUNICATION. Can he communicate on different interpersonal levels depending upon with whom he is communicating? Is he careful with his communication or does he have a "big mouth?" Is he an effective listener? Does he speak and write with proper grammar, vocabulary, and pronunciation? Does he practice not saying anything too stupid? Does he write neatly and literately?

16. ETIQUETTE and GOOD MANNERS. Does he behave when in front of polite company? Is he courteous and respectful, especially, when communicating to parents, grandparents, teachers, and all Adults? Does he use "Sir" when talking to a Man, and "Ma'am" when addressing a Woman? Can he shake hands and greet people properly? Does he use profanity in public? Does he greet everyone he meets or passes on the street with a "good morning," or "good afternoon," or some other simple acknowledgement of that other person's presence? Does he, when passing another Man, make brief eye contact, acknowledge the contact with a simple greeting or a head nod of recognition?

17. PROFICIENT STUDENT. Is he an excellent student? Does he always study hard and perform well in his training and education? Is he a polite and respectful student? Does he stay out of trouble at school? Does he know how to prepare for school, how to enroll in college or trade school, and what

is required to graduate? If he is going to college, will his education lead to a well-paying job?

18. GOAL SETTING. Does he set, for himself, short, medium, and long term goals? Does he write them down? Does he usually accomplish his goals?

19. CITIZENSHIP. Is he a loyal and involved citizen? Does he obey the law? Is he a good neighbor? Does he understand how government works? Does he know who his elected representatives are? Does he perform community service in some form? Did he register to vote on his 18th birthday?

20. DRIVING/DRIVER LICENSE/TRANSPORTATION. Does he have a valid driver's license to operate any standard passenger automobile? Is he a safe and courteous driver? Has he purchased a personal vehicle? Does he keep his vehicle in good mechanical condition? Does he keep his vehicle clean? Does he make all his of vehicle payments on time? Does he have proof of vehicle insurance? Does he keep his vehicle validly registered? Can he use any form of public transportation? Can he travel by air or rail, including planning the travel, scheduling, and purchasing tickets? Does he ride and take care of a bike?

21. GIRLS AND COURTSHIP. Is he clear as to his courtship mission: to find the perfect woman to be his Wife; and mother of his children? Does he know how to be polite and charming, making the women around him feel comfortable and secure? Can he properly court and woo a woman? Does he know how to approach and meet females? How to make them happy? Does he know what qualities he wants in a wife? Has he learned all he can about women: how they think; their behavior patterns; and why they act the way they do? Does he understand the fundamental steps of courtship? Does he understand the species Homo Sapiens' mating biology? Does he understand his biological mating mission and hers?

22. USING COMMUNICATION DEVICES. Does he properly and courteously use all electronic communication methods and devices: telephones, internet, email, texting, and, of course, social media? Does he communicate properly using any device he has mastered? Is he literate; able to speak, read, and write English with enough skill that he is understood and he can understand others who speak English? Does he use

good manners while communicating, and is courteous and respectful? Does he know how to type on all keyboards he uses? Is he respectful of others by not disturbing them while using a communication device? Does he realize there is no privacy in cyberspace? He is careful as to what communication he puts out there? Can he obtain a cell phone, get high speed internet, buy and use a computer? He can email and text?

23. MANAGING FINANCES. Does he know how to make money? Does he manage his money? Does he have a financial plan? Does he use and properly manage his bank accounts? His ATM/Debit card? His credit card? Does he pay off his credit card balance every month? Does he balance and reconcile all bank accounts monthly? Can he start and manage an investment/retirement account? Does he use computer software to manage his personal finances? Does he prepare and file his own federal and state tax returns? Can he submit scholarship and student loan paperwork? Does he understand basic economics: stock markets, Federal Reserve, GDP, inflation, banking, marketplace, deficit spending, etc? Does he maintain good credit and FICO score? Does he maintain proper cash flow? Does he pay all his bills on time?

24. PET/ANIMAL OWNERSHIP AND CARE. Does he take care of all animals he is responsible for, every day? Does he assess the number and types of pets he can responsibly manage? Does he enjoy all the animals in his care?

25. WORK/FIND A JOB. Does he have a work ethic? Can he always find a paying job, in an environment that pays well, and that he enjoys? Does he figure out what job he wants, networks it, trains for it, then applies, interviews, and gets hired? Does he know how to keep a job? Is he a reliable worker?

26. FIND A PLACE TO LIVE. Does he accurately calculate his cost of living budget? Does he locate suitable housing on or under his budget? Does he complete all lease/rental agreements? Does he obtain and maintain renters insurance? Does he keep his home clean and in good order? Does he obtain utilities, including internet, cable/satellite TV, gas, electric, etc? Does he maintain a professional relationship with his landlord and his neighbors? Does he know how to buy a house?

27. LIFE/CAREER PLANNING. Does he have a life career plan? Does he know where he is going in life, at least in the first 4 to

7 years?

28. SPIRITUALITY. Does he have some spirituality in him? Has he found something to fill his spiritual needs?

29. QUIBBLING. Does he whine or quibble? Does he make excuses for his failures?

30. STRESS and ANGER MANAGEMENT. Does he stay cool and calm when it hits the fan? Does he control his anger? Is he patient and able to bring calmness, not add stress? Does he use stress relievers like boxing, martial arts or meditation?

31. BORROWING and LOANING. When he borrows someone else's property, does he always return it on time in the same condition (or better) than when he got it? If he loses or damages other person's property, does he quickly offer an apology and pay for a replacement or repair? Does he loan his property only to other Men, not to a boy unless properly supervised? If he loans money, is he clear on the terms, payment due dates and amount? Or does he make it clear to the borrower that he intends to give that money away as a gift with no expectation of payback?

32. PROPERTY MANAGEMENT. Does he respect and take care of his personal property (from clothes to a car to a house) and the property of others he is responsible for? Does he keep track of his property, keep it in good working order and replace it as needed? Does he minimize hoarding and pack ratting?

33. LIBIDO MANAGEMENT. Does he manage his libido? Does he practice certain techniques that enable him to keep his libido under control?

34. TIME MANAGEMENT. Does he organize his time so he can get done what needs doing, and maybe have some spare time to enjoy life? Does he use a written schedule and some type of clock to track time, to not miss appointments?

35. TEAMWORK. Is he a loyal team member and competent team leader? Does he join some type of team: sports, scouts, recreational, military, work, etc? Does he put the needs of his teammates before his own needs? Is he mission-focused?

36. GOOD DECISION MAKING. Does he make good decisions ... most of the time? Does he have good judgment and common sense; have that ability to make a decision objectively, authoritatively, and wisely, especially in serious or consequential matters? Does he usually make some decision,

good or bad, rather than none at all? Does he practice making good decisions under various situations and time constraints?

37. RELATIONSHIP MANAGEMENT. Does he consider all of his relationships to be important and worthy of his time? Does he cultivate and maintain his relationships? Is his personal philosophy to give more of himself and to expect less from others in maintaining and managing healthy relationships? Does he stay in touch?

38. A MORAL COMPASS. Does he have a moral compass? Does he clearly know the difference between wrong and wrong, good and bad?

39. LEADERSHIP and FOLLOWERSHIP. Is he an effective and competent leader, who can build and lead a cohesive team? Is he a loyal "follower" and team member, one who can be counted on do his part to accomplish the team's mission? Is he ever a "control freak" or an incompetent leader?

40. PROFESSIONAL ASSHOLE. Is he a "Professional Asshole?" Is he, on the rare occasion when he must be, an amateur asshole until what needs doing is done? Then, does he revert back to his normal courteous, kind and caring demeanor? Does he understand the different types of assholes, "Professional vs. Amateur?"

SCORING,
MANHOOD TEST #1 — ADULT, 5th Ed.

- **400 (100%) thru 380 (95%)—PASS.** Perfect. He is an Adult, and a Man. He has mastered all the Adult skills. He is ready to learn to teach other males to be Adults. Ladies, this is the Man you will want to marry if he passes all his other Manhood tests.

- **379 (94%) thru 360 (90%)—PASS.** He is an Adult, but needs some polish on a few of the Adult skills to score higher if you want a perfect Man. Ladies, this Man is just about perfect. So, you may be the type of Woman who likes a dash of bad boy mixed in her perfect Man type. And you will fall in love with him.

- **359 (89%) thru 320 (80%)—FAIL.** More boy than Man. Remedial training required on many Adult skills.

- **319 (79%) thru 280 (70%)—FAIL.** He's a little baby. He could try to master the Adult skills, but maybe does not want to put out the effort. He is probably very happy and comfortable living the spoiled brat lifestyle, preferring that his mommy takes care of him.

- **279 (69%) thru 240 (60%)—FAIL.** Definitely a boy who may never make Manhood. Chronically infected with P-Syndrome. May not be curable. Most likely got zero points in several adult skills, low points in others, and needs immediate remedial training in most of the skills.

- **239 (59%) thru 0 (0%)—FAIL.** 100% candy-ass, little baby. This guy has terminal PS that will eventually kill him. He is a first class loser who has chosen to be a baby. He does not intend to master any of the adult skills, thus has no chance to achieve adulthood and be a Man. His best career move is to become an organ donor. Somebody eventually will put a bullet in his head or shank him in prison.

* * * * *

The Mission of Adulthood is to be a contributing member of society, enjoying life, liberty, and the pursuit of happiness. The foundation of what it means to be a Man starts at Adulthood.

Citizen, Husband, and Father all develop from a solid foundation of mature and responsible adulthood. If a male does not succeed as an Adult, it will be impossible for him to go forward, and take on the other duties of a Man.

From mature and responsible Adult, the next duty of a Man is to be a loyal and involved Citizen.

CHAPTER 4

LOYAL AND INVOLVED CITIZEN

"All worthwhile men have good thoughts, good ideas, and good intentions—
but precious few ever translate those into action."
— *John Hancock Field*

"Every good citizen makes his country's honor his own,
and cherishes it not only as precious but as sacred.
He is willing to risk his life in its defence
and is conscious that he gains protection while he gives it."
— *Andrew Jackson, US President*

The second of four duties of a Man is a loyal and involved citizen. One of the behavioral traits of Homo Sapiens is this species tend to live in tribes and groups. Because we are a diametric species, capable of good and evil, we must train our youngsters early on as to how they fit into our tribe, our society, as good citizens. We teach them how to get along with the other members of the tribe. We teach them how to do their part to contribute to the welfare of the tribe. A loyal and involved Citizen is just that. He takes care of his people and he helps society as best he can, for the greater good of his community. Because a Man wants to live and raise his family in a happy, positive, thriving society.

As with Adult, the male must master the citizenship skills needed then pass the test. Trainers should start running the skills checklist when the boy is school age. He should take Manhood Test #2 — Citizen, at the same time as he is tested for Adult, or up to a year after he passes the Adult Test.

How does a Man accomplish the duties of "loyal and involved Citizen?" Here is the skill list. As with the adult skills, I am sure my list is not complete. However, it is enough to be able to accomplish the duties of a Man as a Citizen. As with the adult skills, some of the citizen skills are easy to understand. Below I list each citizen skill with a breakdown of tasks within that skill, and, if needed, a brief explanation of what "mastering" the skill looks like.

SKILLS CHECKLIST — CITIZEN, 3rd Ed.

1. Loyal Citizen
2. Involved Citizen
3. Obeys the Law
4. Respects Authority
5. Speaks English
6. Understands Basic Government
7. Respects Community
8. Stands Up for Rights
9. Cross Culturalism
10. Votes
11. Community Service
12. Knows Who Is Running the Government
13. Constitution
14. Knows What's Going on in the World
15. Good Neighbor
16. Code of Conduct
17. Member of Professional Organization
18. Support the Military
19. Noble Cause

Now, the skills in detail. Followed by the test.

CITIZEN SKILL #1 — LOYAL CITIZEN

- A Man is a loyal citizen. Loyalty is a fundamental character trait. A Man is faithful to his sovereign, government, and/ or state. He is faithful to his oaths, vows, commitments, promises, and obligations. And a Man is faithful to his leader, his party, or his cause, or to any person or thing conceived of as deserving of his giving of his word.

We are slow to recognize loyalty in others. Most humans can be loyal to something. Loyalty is what makes a team successful. It also keeps families together. It is the stuff that keeps the military on point and on mission around the world.

- A Man would never, ever, become a traitor to his country, his family, or his word.

Treason, in my opinion, is the one crime worthy of the death penalty by firing squad. Traitors who have sold secrets and spied for our enemies have damaged—many times irreparably— America's ability to defend itself and protect its citizens, while abetting our enemies ability to do us harm. To a greater extent, the dishonorable actions of those turncoats instigated the capture, torture, and death of American military personnel and intelligence officers, as well as the compromise of our most sensitive secrets. Shoot them all!

CITIZEN SKILL #2 — INVOLVED CITIZEN

- A Man is an involved citizen.

The foundation of a democracy is its citizens. In the United States, the cornerstone on which this great nation was built is embodied in the Constitution, establishing the basis for citizen involvement in governance.

The right and responsibility of citizenship unfolds in many ways. Citizen involvement in governance encompasses not only citizen participation (through mechanisms such as public hearings) but also citizen decision making, information sharing, and voting. Citizen involvement is important for local governments worldwide because it increases legitimacy, efficiency, and accountability, and because it distributes the burden of good governance among all citizens, not just local government officials.

The methods of citizen involvement range from dissemination of information through electronic networks, newsletters, and public meetings, to engaged and participatory processes (such as strategic planning, task forces, public meetings, and focus groups) that encourage all citizens to be active players in decisions made for their community.

CITIZEN SKILL #3 — OBEY THE LAW

- A Man obeys the law.
- His obedience philosophy is called "spirit-of-the-law."

He recognizes the purpose of law is to bring good order to a society. And to establish rules for self-control and to protect the rights of all citizens in a civilization. Laws keep citizens safe and bring some order to a society. They define good and bad behavior.

Rarely do all citizens obey every single law on the books. My disobedience tends to be violations of the vehicle code. I tend to drive a little fast. And I may not come to a full and complete stop at every single stop sign. I don't wear a seat belt while driving. Could I flunk my own test? Depends on whether you believe in the competing philosophies of obedience called, "the-spirit-of-the-law" or "the-letter-of-the-law." When one believes in the literal interpretation of the words (the "letter") of the law, that person would stop at every single stop sign, even if its in the middle of nowhere, at 4 a.m. in the morning, and not a human for 30 miles. A "letter-of-the-law" person would drive the speed limit everywhere at all times, and would always wear their seat belt. Sounds like a good philosophy doesn't it? Not to me. A "letter-of-the-law" man would be a 100% by-the-book rule enforcement officer. If this man was responsible to discipline others, he would show no mercy. To a man with this philosophy, he believes there are no gray areas, no leniency or forgiveness for bad decisions. They only see in black and white.

> "No slack, at no time, to no one."
> — Anonymous Police Field Training Officer

I think all Men should believe in the far more flexible "spirit-of-the-law" philosophy. There is a big grey area in the middle of this belief; black on the right and white on the left. I obey the spirit of the law, but not the letter, doing what the author of the rule, policy, or law intended, though not necessarily adhering to the literal wording. Traffic laws where put on the books to make the roads safer and prevent accidents. I would never speed through a school zone crowded with children. I may speed if it is 4:30 a.m. in the morning and heading home from work. I drive about 20 (in a 25 mph zone) in my neighborhood during the day and maybe a little faster late at night. I will drive 75 to 90 on the freeway in light traffic. I stop at all stop signs where other cars or pedestrians are present. But I roll through empty intersections when I am all alone. As a military officer I was a "spirit-of-the-law" type of leader. The military tended to better accomplish its mission in the gray area. Troops break the rules. Depending on the circumstances, a little mercy may be the best punishment for disobedience.

"Obedience is the mother of success and is wedded to safety"
— Aeschylus

Don't overlook what I said earlier. The "spirit-of-the-law" philosophy does have some black and white. Sometimes the guy has to go to jail or the brig for his disobedience. But there must be some mercy to temper punishment. I am a pretty forgving guy. However, you can tell I get pretty black and white over traitors. Especially the ones whose treason got some of my comrades killed. No mercy to them.

So, am I disobedient enough to flunk my own citizenship test? I don't believe so. Your the judge. And if you are administering the citizen test to a guy trying to be a Man, you will have to decide if he passes this skill or not.

"This is the very perfection of a man,
to find out his own imperfections."
— Saint Augustine, Ancient Roman Theologian

CITIZEN SKILL #4 — RESPECTS AUTHORITY

- A Man respects authority. He respects any boss because he knows that boss is responsible for something to the bigger boss.

We men respect our military, our police/fire/EMS, our courts and our government. We respect teachers, doctors, and clergy.

If those groups become disrespectful, then it is a citizen's job to do something to fix the problem. Maybe the police were out of line. A Citizen will say something.

Also too, a Man will publicly recognize and praise those we respect. I have personally written letters to military commanders and to police chiefs praising their people for getting the job done in a professional manner. We are quick to condemn bad behavior, and too slow to praise good behavior.

CITIZEN SKILL #5 — SPEAKS ENGLISH

- If the Man's home is America, he can speak, read, and write in English fluently enough to fulfill his duties as a Man.

India has over two dozen official languages and 600 dialects. The Philippines have over half a dozen official languages and hundreds of dialects. What these two countries have in common is their official language is English, their language of government, media, academia, and corporations. English provides them a common language to communicate.

English is the de facto national language of the United States, with 82% of the population claiming it as a mother tongue, and some 96% claiming to speak it well. However, no official language exists at the federal level. (U.S. CENSUS)

Even though over 30 states have declared English their official language, we are unwilling to declare English federally out of fear of being politically incorrect, ignorantly believing we will offend our ethnically diverse population. Instead of it being an insult to ethnicity, it is a bonus if we can all speak the same language to take care of business as Adults and Citizens; it will help all of us live better. Say we had another hurricane or tornado type of natural disaster. Would it not assist the rescuers and the disaster victims if they could speak the same language? Would it not help the police directing an evacuation of the disaster area if the cops and the evacuees speak the same language?

One reason I love America is its rich ethnic diversity. We never want to lose any of those cultures. My reason for putting this skill on the list is with no disrespect intended. This skill helps us, as a community, to be able to communicate on common ground. If India and The Philippines can do it, America should be able to. Are we that mired in political correctness?

CITIZEN SKILL #6 — UNDERSTANDS BASIC GOVERNMENT

- A Man understands the basic structure of federal, state, and local Government. And how they work.
- He can pass the United States of America Citizenship Test.

The Citizenship test is administered to all immigrants who want to become U.S. citizens. About 92% of the people who take the citizenship test pass on their first try, according to immigration service data.

However, Newsweek recently gave 1,000 Americans the U.S. Citizenship test and found that their knowledge of the history and running of their own country was seriously lacking. Only 38% of Americans passed and some didn't know answers to basic questions like who is the vice president? The questions that Americans could not answer went from the more challenging, like, how many justices are in the Supreme Court (63% didn't know), to the most basic, like, who is the vice president of America (29% didn't know). An alarming number of Americans did not know basic information about the Constitution, namely that it was the supreme law of the land, that it was set up at the Constitutional Convention and that the first ten amendments are known as the Bill of Rights. (QUIGLEY)

CITIZEN SKILL #7 — RESPECTS COMMUNITY

- A Man treats his community, and its members, with respect and courtesy.

A man does not drive 50 miles per hour through a school zone. He is polite and courteous to all members of his community. He makes all feel welcome.

- A Man keeps community clean. He does not litter and he picks up after the lazy slobs who do.

Keeping the community clean is nearly as important as obeying the law. All community members should take pride in their community by at least keeping it clean. Maybe a community service project could be to paint the park benches or pick up all of the trash.

CITIZEN SKILL #8 — STANDS UP FOR RIGHTS

• A Man is willing to fight for his rights and the rights of others.

Sometimes a Citizen has to stand against an injustice, great or small. Maybe it's fighting city hall to have a new bike lane put into your neighborhood so the kids will have a safe place to ride their bikes. Maybe you are moved to action because of what you read in this book about female genitalia mutilation in Africa, or about abuse of women in general. A Man does something more than just complain, especially if he observes that someone's rights are being violated.

CITIZEN SKILL #9 — CROSS CULTURALISM

- A Man understands, respects, and enjoys the cultural and ethnic similarities and differences among those who live here.
- A Man actually enjoys and revels in cultural and ethnic diversity.

I find other humans fascinating. It's the reason I became a cultural anthropologist. I love to eat the food from around the world. I enjoy world music, be it African drums or Egyptian rap music. America is blessed with such a diverse culture that exists nowhere else on the planet. A Man welcomes and embraces cross culturalism.

CITIZEN SKILL #10 — VOTES

- A Man is always registered to vote in his home state and county, no matter where he is in the world.
- He votes in all elections, either at the polling place or by mail-in ballot. He takes the time to study the candidates and propositions so he may vote wisely.
- He is a member of a political party. He may even work or contribute to a political campaign.

> "You can't bitch if you don't vote."
> — Anonymous voter

If you don't vote, you don't have a right to complain about what is wrong with the government. To me, the phrase means more than just voting; you shouldn't complain about a situation until you've done everything in your power to change it.

CITIZEN SKILL #11 — COMMUNITY SERVICE

- A Man participates in some form of community service in his local neighborhood, his state, or his country.

Civic participation is not required in the United States. There is no requirement to attend town meetings, read newspapers, stay informed about issues, belong to a political party, or write letters; citizens can stay home and do nothing if they so choose.

A Man will volunteer at the local library to read to kids. He will help out with any number of charitable organizations. He will serve as a Boy Scout Leader or a member of a church group. He will join the military or a volunteer fire department. All are good ways to serve.

CITIZEN SKILL #12 — KNOWS
WHO IS RUNNING GOVERNMENT

- A Man knows who all of the government key players are: local, state, and federal representatives/public officials.
- A Man knows some members of government personally from networking as an involved Citizen.

Who is his county sheriff, his governor, his Secretary of Defense? He knows who they all are.

CITIZEN SKILL #13 — CONSTITUTION

- A Man has read the U.S. Constitution, the Bill of Rights, and the Declaration of Independence.

He should also have read his state constitution and his local city or county charter/bylaws. A Man knows what government is supposed to be doing as defined by their constitutions and charters. He knows how he can hold his elected officials' feet to the fire if they are violating the law or the Constitution.

CITIZEN SKILL #14 — KNOWS
WHAT'S GOING ON IN THE WORLD

- A Man knows what is going on in the world.
- He reads and watches the news, stays informed of world, regional, and local news events.
- He pays attention to what governments are up to, and the geopolitics of the world's hot spots, and how it all fits together globally and here at home.

The President gets his morning briefing every day. A Man can do the same. At the beginning of the day, he can read over a selection of different world, national, and local news sources, all now online. All news organizations tend to be bias to the right or left. What I don't like about American news organizations is they tend to focus nearly all their attention on the United States. While it is important to know what the news is in America, you need to really stay up on the world news as we are globally interconnected.

As of the day I wrote this, 18 Feb 2012, the European Union, mostly Britain and France, initiated economic sanctions against Iran because that nation is trying to build nuclear weapons. Since Iran is an OPEC country, how will the sanctions impact the price of oil and gasoline here at home? You need to know that. Now it's 10 March. The price of a gallon of gas in Sacramento as skyrocketed to well over $4.00.

For world news, I like Reuters News Service and BBC News. National news, I like the New York Times, Fox News, and NPR as a good balance. The Drudge Report is good for political news. I read the Sacramento Bee and watch KCRA, Channel 3, for my local news and weather.

CITIZEN SKILL #15 — GOOD NEIGHBOR

- A Man is a good neighbor. He personally knows his neighbors.
- He is helpful to his neighbors and protective of his neighborhood.

Depending on how much space exists between homes, the level of friendliness with the neighbors will vary. One of the cornerstone traits of being an American is our individuality and privacy. We want to know enough about our neighbors to be cordial and safe, avoiding getting too much into any neighbor's business. I want to know enough about my neighbors to safeguard the neighborhood and to look out for each other.

I live in Sacramento, California, a city of about 400,000. My neighborhood is called Land Park; it's mostly single-family homes built from the 1920s through the 1960s. Big trees down the street and in the yards. I have lived in this neighborhood off and on for 40 years. I know all of the neighbors living next to me and across the street from me, by name. And I know some neighbors who live next to my neighbors. That's it. My brother-in-law and his wife live in the mountains on 160 acres. They know all of their neighbors within 20 miles of their ranch.

CITIZEN SKILL #16 — CODE OF CONDUCT

- A Man lives by a code of conduct, a set of rules outlining responsibilities and good behavior for a Man.

There are all types of codes of conduct published by government organizations, religious groups, and professional organizations. The 10 Commandments is a code of conduct. The Hippocratic Oath is a code of conduct.

Even my definition of a Man can be a code of conduct: a mature and responsible adult, loyal and involved citizen, loving and faithful husband, and patient and caring father.

If a Man lives by his good character, he is living by a code of conduct.

CITIZEN SKILL #17 — MEMBER OF PROFESSIONAL ORGANIZATION

- A Man is a member of a professional organization.

Some examples include the Rotarians, Promise Keepers, American Legion, Elks, NAACP, etc. Also a Man can be a member of a church, civic, vet, or private group with a community service mission.

You can knock out several skills at once by joining a professional organization like the Chamber of Commerce, Rotarians, or Elks. The Rotarians do community service; they work on being good neighbors, and a good source of career networking.

CITIZEN SKILL #18 — SUPPORT THE MILITARY

- A Man supports the military.

All men should serve in one of the five branches of the armed forces: Army, Navy, Air Force, Marine Corps, or Coast Guard. One can serve full time on active duty for three or four years, then collect that $65,000.00 college GI Bill. Or a Man can serve part time in the Reserves or the National Guard component of one of the five military services. Less than 30% of first time enlistees stay in for a 20 to 30 year career like I did. The military is not every man's career lifestyle. Not all of us Men are cut out to be professional warriors.

If he does not or cannot serve in the military, a Man is an avid supporter of the men and women in uniform, as well as of the military veterans. A Man understands that freedom is not free. It is paid for with the blood of our soldiers, sailor, airman, and marines.

> The tree of liberty must be refreshed from time to time,
> with the blood of patriots and tyrants.
> It is its natural manure.
> — Thomas Jefferson

CITIZEN SKILL #19 — NOBLE CAUSE

- A Man engages in a noble cause.

He takes on some gallant action for the greater good of his community, country, and/or society. A man undertakes a noble cause to leave something good of himself behind when he is gone, for the betterment of life.

A (noble or) transcendental cause is an action that a Man believes is truly heroic (a noble endeavor calling for bravery and self-sacrifice), timeless (has significance beyond the moment), and is supremely meaningful (not futile). (LEWIS)

I know that sounds like a Man has to slay a dragon or save the whales or something. It's simply something that burns inside of a Man to leave his mark in a positive way. He wants to know he can bring a little good to others for no other reason than it feels good to help others.

I started by noble cause in 1970 when I joined the United States Army. I was 17, trying to stay out of juvenile hall. The Army was the only service that would take me. 26 years later I retired as a

Captain in the Air Force. My cause was to defend my country. I was a warrior ... a sheep dog, watching over the sheep so the wolves didn't eat them.

After the military came my new cause, in the world of police and military working dogs. Bomb dogs in particular. My mission was to safeguard the young men and women who were explosive detection (bomb) dog handlers, and their dogs; protecting them as they walk in harm's way to make us safe. That little working dog world was fragmented into different egotistical kingdoms and narcissistic fiefdoms from the different branches of the military, state and local police agencies, federal law enforcement organizations, and private sector professional working dog companies.

All of the different factions had their own way of training, testing, and working their dog teams. If there were to ever be a massive, terrorist bomb threat, where 20 bomb dog teams were needed, most would not be able to work together because they trained using over 40 forty different standards. What our country needed was just one unified training and testing standard for all dog teams. I was a member of an FBI and National Institute of Justice scientific working group called SWGDOG. We were able to, with great resistance from the various kingdoms and fiefdoms, hammer out America's first truly national standard for bomb dog teams. Creating that unified training, testing, and operations model was my noble cause. I feel I have helped the handlers and dogs be safer working in such a dangerous environment.

My work on that dog mission was accomplished about 2008. From there I spent about a year searching for my next noble cause. It turns out that it was writing this book. My new mission is to spread the word that manhood is declining. I have decided that I want to beat "the awareness and call-to-action drum" to demand your attention to this catastrophe. We have to help our boys become Men, to achieve true Manhood.

So, the male being tested on this, the noble cause, is being asked an "all or none" question. He is actively planning, doing, or finishing a cause, or not. He gets either ten points or zero points.

MANHOOD TEST #2 — CITIZEN, 3rd Ed.

Once all the training is completed, the next step is Manhood Test #2 — Citizen.

NOTE: Once the infrastructure is in place the man being tested must have passed the adult test beforehand, and possess a valid man card. No exceptions.

The test is administered by a minimum of three adults, who have intimate knowledge of the male's training and preparation for citizenship. Test administrators should include a combination of parents, teachers, clergy, or elders. The Man being assessed should be present in case a test administrator wishes to ask the boy any questions.

Administer this test periodically before the boy turns 18 to determine where his weak areas are for further training. The official test is taken between 17 ½ and 19 ½ years old. If he fails the Citizen test, he must participate in remedial training. Once he has been deemed ready to take the test again, the entire examination will be administered once more.

DIRECTIONS TO TEST ADMINISTRATOR:
1. Read all 19 questions.
2. Score each question 0 to 10 points.
3. Total the score (190 points maximum).
4. Use the scoring chart at the end of the test to determine the final results and the status of the tested male.

SCORING TIPS: You can score each question from zero (0) to a maximum of ten (10) points. When evaluating the question, consider whether or not the male you are testing has 100% succeeded on a particular question; that's 10 points. If he is near perfect then that is an 8 or 9. If the guy is missing a important part of the skill, that is 3 to 7 points. If he is nearly failing, that is 1 or 2 points. And finally, if this guy you're testing is clueless on a skill, or just totally failing, that is ZERO points. Your objectivity comes into play. The bottom line is your scoring will determine if this guy is an Adult and a Citizen ... or not. Be hard, be ruthless in your scoring. We cannot allow any male who is not ready to slip through.

Mastering Citizen skills and passing the second Manhood Test is a rite-of-passage. If you pass a Man, and he fails to perform as a Citizen, you may have to explain why you passed him. The test must take years to prepare for and be difficult, but not impossible, to pass. Remember, no matter how hard we train and mentor, preparing our boys for the test, some guys were just never meant to be Citizens. A certain percentage will be chronic failures for a variety of reasons.

19 multipart questions. 10 points each. 190 points total.

1. LOYAL CITIZEN. Is the Man a loyal citizen? Is he faithful to his country, his promises and commitments, and anyone he gives his word to? Is he a traitor?
2. INVOLVED CITIZEN. Is the Man an involved citizen? Does he step up to help his community and his country?
3. OBEY THE LAW. Does the Man obey the law? Does he have a "spirit-of-the-law" philosophy?
4. RESPECTS AUTHORITY. Does the Man respect authority?
5. SPEAKS ENGLISH. Does the Man speak, read, and write English fluently enough to fulfill his duties as a Man?
6. UNDERSTANDS BASIC GOVERNMENT. Does the Man understand the basic structure of Federal, State, and local Government and how they work? If applicable, has he taken and passed the Citizenship Test?
7. RESPECTS COMMUNITY. Does the Man treat his community, and its members, with respect and courtesy? Does he keep his community clean? Does he litter?
8. STANDS UP FOR RIGHTS. Does the Man stand up for his rights and the rights of others?
9. CROSS CULTURALISM. Does the Man understand, respect, and enjoy the cultural and ethnic similarities and differences among those who live here?
10. VOTES. Is the Man registered to vote no matter where he is in the world? Does he vote in all elections? Is he a member of a political party?
11. COMMUNITY SERVICE. Does the Man participate in some

form of community service in his local neighborhood, his state, or his country?

12. KNOWS WHO IS RUNNING THE GOVERNMENT. Does the Man know who all the government key players are: local, state, and federal representatives/public officials?

13. CONSTITUTION. Has the Man read the U.S. Constitution, Bill of Rights, and Declaration of Independence? Does he understand the significance of those documents?

14. KNOWS WHAT'S GOING ON IN THE WORLD. Does he know what is going on in the world? Does he read the news, and keep informed of world, regional, and local news events? Does he pay attention to government and geopolitics?

15. GOOD NEIGHBOR. Is the Man a good neighbor? Does he personally know his neighbors? Is he helpful to his neighbors and protective of his neighborhood?

16. CODE OF CONDUCT. Does the Man live by a code of conduct? Does he have a set of rules outlining responsibilities and good behavior for a Man?

17. MEMBER OF PROFESSIONAL ORGANIZATION. Is the Man a member of a professional organization?

18. SUPPORT THE MILITARY. Does the Man support the military?

19. NOBLE CAUSE. Does the Man engage in a noble cause?

SCORING, MANHOOD TEST #2 — CITIZEN, 3ʳᵈ Ed.

- **190 (100%) thru 180 (95%)—PASS.** Perfect. He is a loyal and involved Citizen. He has mastered all the Citizen skills.

- **179 (94%) thru 171 (90%)—PASS.** He is a Citizen with just a touch of rebelliousness. Needs only some polish on a few of the citizen skills to make him perfect.

- **170 (89%) thru 152 (80%)—FAIL.** Probably did not pass the Adult test either. Remedial training required on many citizen skills.

- **151 (79%) thru 133 (70%)—FAIL.** He's a welfare recipient. He could try to master the citizen skills, but he probably has not passed the Adult test. He is probably very happy and comfortable living off the taxpayers.

- **132 (69%) thru 114 (60%)—FAIL.** Definitely on government assistance. A boy who may never make manhood. Chronically infected with PS. May not be curable. Most likely flunked the Adult test more than once.

- **113 (59%) thru 0 (0%)—FAIL.** This guy is a homeless drug addict ... by choice since his parents had to throw him out of the house because of his chronic unemployment and drug addiction.

* * * * *

The Mission of Citizenship is to be an Adult in the community. To be a loyal and involved member of that society.

So, let's say the boy passed the Adult and Citizen tests. He is a Man and an Adult who, for the next few years, should be executing the life/career plan he worked on for his Adult test. Then, he either goes in the military, or he gets a "good enough" job until he can get trained and educated for the really good, well-paying job in a career field he will enjoy. Then, he needs to start looking for a wife. It will take him some time to find the right woman.

Regarding finding a wife, the next chapters contain the skills to master, and the tests to take, after which he will be able to get picked by a good woman who wants to fall in love and marry him.

CHAPTER 5

"PRE-HUSBAND"

"What is the difference between men and women?
A woman wants one man to satisfy her every need.
A man wants every woman to satisfy his one need."
— *Anonymous*

In my house I'm the boss, my wife is just the decision maker."
— *Woody Allen.*

This chapter focuses on the point in a Man's life where he has passed the Adult and Citizen tests. He is executing his life/career plan he wrote for his adult test. The Man is probably in the military, at some other full time work, or is getting educated and trained for the well-paid job he is preparing for.

Now is the time in a Man's life/career plan to start looking for his Wife.

As I mentioned in chapter 3, the biological reproductive mission of Homo sapien males is to input his genetic material in as many human females as he can in his lifetime. The human females' reproductive mission is to select the perfect male from among the array of males desiring to mate with her.

A male human wants to mate with every human female. A female human wants to marry and mate with the one perfect human male. To increase the odds of being "picked," a Man must master what I call "Pre-Husband" skills. There is a period in a Man's life between Adult and Citizen, and Husband that I call the "pre-husband" period. This is where the bulk of courtship takes place with the mission of finding a good woman to marry. Female humans are not well trained to select that one perfect man to marry. Women seem to pick a husband candidate by pure emotion.

From Chapter 3, here is a review of the ritual of mate selection typically used by human females from more developed western cultures. The steps, as told to me by a wonderful lady named Jackie S., go something like this:

1. "First I meet this guy. He seems to be a keeper. He is big, strong, charming, and handsome. He makes me laugh and feel good. I'm thinking that I hope I don't fall in love with him too fast."
2. "Then, I realize, oh shoot, too late, I love him."
3. "But, wait, he is turning out to be a bastard who takes my money, cheats on me, and makes me cry a lot."
4. "No problem, I can fix him like Mom fixed Dad. We women have been training our men for decades."
5. "Oh man, I give up. I really can't fix him."
6. "Now, my heart is broken and I have to leave him, the man I fell in love with. Damn!"
7. "Next, I go back to step 1 and repeat with the next guy I fall in love with. Once I get my heart broken a few more times, I will slip into my emotionally dark place, to become a jealous, unloved, man-hating, lesbian, psycho bitch!"

> "Insanity is repeating the same mistakes,
> and expecting different results."
> — Narcotics Anonymous Manual

If I were to systematize Jackie's Husband selection process, her steps in "Man selection" would look something like this.

HOW WOMEN PICK A BAD BOY
by Jackie S.

1. See bad boy. He is handsome, charming, and funny.
2. Pick bad boy. Reasons listed in step 1.
3. Fall in love with bad boy.
4. Realize bad boy is a bastard.
5. Attempt to "fix" bad boy to make him a Man.
6. Can't fix; dump bad boy.
7. Begin weeping, sobbing, and blubbering while eating chocolate.
8. Become gloomy, dejected, disappointed, and miserable.
9. Recover emotionally just enough to stupidly repeat step 1.
10. Continue repeating bad boy selection process until the loss of all self-esteem, guilt, failure, and depression causes her to change from a beautiful, intelligent, and happy Woman, to a man-hating, unloved, psycho lesbian, with a chocolate addiction.

Girls, as part of their adult training, must be taught to pick the best Man logically, as well as emotionally. They must use both logic and emotion to make the correct Husband selection.

Poor choice of a husband candidate, I hypothesize, is the reason America's outrageous divorce rate for "first time marrieds" ranges from 40% to 60%. The pre-husband test will reduce that up front guesswork in picking out the perfect husband candidate by evoking her logical side via the test questions. If the guy she is thinking of marrying passes the Pre-Husband Test at 95% or better, I believe the marriage has at least an 80% chance of going the distance (till death do you part).

There is some overlap of skills with Adult and Husband. This test is no less essential, but is supplemental to the Manhood Test series.

If a man passes the Pre-Husband Test at 95%, my instructions to the woman administering the test is to "Marry him immediately." Right now there are few "95%ers" out there. As with previous skill checklists in the book, I list each skill with a breakdown of tasks within that skill, and if needed, add a brief explanation of what "mastering" the skill looks like. Again, email me if you have any suggestions to make this list more complete and accurate, gallantry@lanset.com.

SKILLS CHECKLIST — PRE-HUSBAND 1st Ed.

1. Have a job.
2. True love
3. Committed Relationship
4. Fatherhood and Children
5. Neat and Clean
6. Personality
7. Money
8. Sex
9. Education and Intelligence
10. Friendship
11. Communication
12. Low Maintenance
13. Common Interests
14. Family and Friends
15. Good Character
16. Mommy and "Exs"
17. Passed Adult and Citizen Manhood Tests
18. Well Mannered
19. Control Freak
20. Spirituality

Now, the skills in detail. Followed by the test.

PRE-HUSBAND SKILL #1 — HAVE A JOB

- A Man supports himself. His job makes enough money.
- A Man has a clear career/life plan that maps out his goals, including how he intends to support himself, and eventually, a wife and kids.

PRE-HUSBAND SKILL #2 — TRUE LOVE

- A man truly loves his woman.

- He makes her happy.
- He makes her feel appreciated and respected for all she does for him.
- A Man realizes, when a Woman tells her Man she loves him, she is giving him her heart, mind, body, and soul. She holds nothing back.

Love is an incredibly powerful word. When a Man is in love, he will always want to be with his Woman. And when a Man is not able to be with her, he dreams of her. Because, until he can be by her side, a Man's life is incomplete.

PRE-HUSBAND SKILL #3 — COMMITTED RELATIONSHIP

- Once the Man finds the right woman to be his Wife, he wants a committed relationship.

A boy wants to hop from female to female in his quest to fulfill his reproductive mission. That is why boys are able to engage in sex in an emotionless and detached manner. It's all about the numbers.

- A Man loves and desires only his Woman. A Man has firm control of his libido. He is on the greater quest to find his queen, his soul mate, his Wife, the mother of his children, the lady he wants to first fall in love with and be committed to.
- A Man wants his Woman to feel that she made the correct decision in picking him as her mate.

PRE-HUSBAND SKILL #4 — FATHERHOOD

- A Man wants to be a Father and have children.

A Man possesses the skills and aptitude necessary to be a patient and caring father. He knows what the difference is between father and daddy. Father is the hard-ass who has to run the family. Daddy is the cool dude who is fun and funny to be with. All wives and kids want Daddy. Nobody wants Father.

PRE-HUSBAND SKILL #5 — NEAT and CLEAN

- The Man must be neat and clean: body, clothing, car, home, work. And well groomed, organized, reliable, and punctual.

If he passed the Manhood Test #1—Adult, he should pass this skill no problem.

PRE-HUSBAND SKILL #6 — PERSONALITY

- A Man's overall personality is usually upbeat, humorous.
- He is rarely moody.
- He can handle stress.

When it hits the fan, a Man does not stress out. In fact, the Man is a calming force in the relationship. For a Man to be cool, he has therapeutic outlets for any stress he has to "suck up" and keep moving. Sex is one outlet. A few times a year, hitting or kicking something for about 15 to 30 minutes is a good stress reliever for Men. I always liked the punching bag. Crashing something, if really stressed out, works but can be pricey. A Man knows how to balance his need for more costly stress relief and the benefit the family gets from a cool-headed dad, not an angry, raging, out-of-control maniac.

Baseball bat versus TV or car is an excellent stress relief exercise.

PRE-HUSBAND SKILL #7 — MONEY

- A Man earns enough money to live decently.
- He manages his money and credit well.
- He has a financial plan.

The adult test has several skills related to money. If he passed the adult test then he will pass this skill with no problem.

PRE-HUSBAND SKILL #8 — SEX

- A Man makes sex fun, satisfying, and stress-free for his Woman.

- He manages his libido very well.

Sex is one of the issues that cause stress and frustration in relationships. Remember the human biological mission. For men, it's all about the numbers. They target as many females as possible to mate with while the female targets "the one," the very best male she can find.

The male humans want all females. The human female wants to "cut" a good Man from the herd. The very best looking, strongest, smartest, richest male she can find.

> "Men want all women for one thing.
> Women want one man for all things."
> — Anonymous

A Man recognizes what his sexual likings are for himself, and he knows what sensual preferences he is looking for in a Woman. Sexual compatibility is important to a long lasting marriage. Especially for a Man. He must know what he likes and does not like. He must pick a Woman who matches his sexual interests. Men get frustrated with their women over sex primarily because Men fail to pick the right sex partner.

A Man in a committed relationship is faithful to his Woman because he understands the Woman picked him to be her Husband. He is done looking. So, he knows to have eyes only for his Woman and no other.

PRE-HUSBAND SKILL #9 — EDUCATION

- A Man is intelligent and educated enough for his Woman.
- A Man considers his Woman to be his intellectual equal, or even his superior. He never makes her feel stupid or intellectually inferior to him.

By "intelligent and educated enough," I mean that for some women a soldier who is a high school graduate is educated enough for her. Other women may wish to marry a Noble prize winning brain surgeon. Some women may be willing to fall in love with a moron.

- A Man has at least graduated from high school. Completing college or a trade school depends on what point he is at on his life/career plan.

PRE-HUSBAND SKILL #10 — FRIENDSHIP

- A Man is emotionally available to his Woman.
- He knows he can trust her to be there for him, for any reason.
- A Man's Woman is his most trusted, best friend. That is essential and crucial; allow me to repeat that. She is his best friend.
- A Man likes people and enjoys the company of others.

PRE-HUSBAND SKILL #11 — COMMUNICATION

- A Man is an effective interpersonal communicator. His Woman will find him genuinely easy to talk with.

This is a skill he mastered to pass the Adult test. An Adult Man is an effective listener. He relies on his Woman to "have his back" by watching out for his character flaws. He gives her the confidence to keep him informed of his flaws. He can take criticism from her without quibbling. He trusts his best friend to criticize him in a kind manner. He trusts her implicitly.

PRE-HUSBAND SKILL #12 — LOW MAINTENANCE

- A Man is "low maintenance," easy to please, and does not require constant pampering and adoration.

It is easy for his Woman to keep him happy. He finds joy in his life. He is genuinely happy, enjoys the company of others, and is easy-going, unselfish and usually a joy to be around.

PRE-HUSBAND SKILL #13 — COMMON INTERESTS

- A Man looks for and enjoys shared common interests with his Woman.

- He shares his interests with her, and she with him, to enjoy the interests together, when and if you both choose to.

My wife and I love to travel and eat the food of foreign lands. We like to ride Harleys, scuba dive, go to movies, and spend time with friends and family.

I like to play with toys like guns, video games, remote control anything, computers, etc. She does not. Pat likes to can jams, salsa, etc. She enjoys cake decorating and experimenting with new recipes. I could care less about cake decorating. But I like to eat cake, salsa, and she makes a to-die-for garlic, veggie pasta sauce that is perfect with her spicy meat balls.

Enjoying international cuisine has been an expanding common interest we still delight in every day, even after 36 years of marriage.

PRE-HUSBAND SKILL #14 — FAMILY and FRIENDS

- The Man's family and friends like and accept, even love, his Woman.

Of course, that should be quid pro quo. Do the Woman's family and friends like and accept the man? His mom likes you? Your dad likes him?

A critical part of the mate selection process is friends and family. In most cultures it is important that the family and friends accept a Man's Woman, and vice versa. If there is any relationship malfunction regarding one family or the other it can contribute to a divorce.

PRE-HUSBAND SKILL #15 — CHARACTER

- He is a Man of good character and he will make an outstanding husband and father.
- He is trustworthily, respectful, fair, caring, self-confident, and kind.

PRE-HUSBAND SKILL #16 — MOMMY and "EXs"

- A Man maintains appropriate professional relationships, as necessary, with his ex-wives (if there are children), baby-mama(s), and his mother.

Do the Math. There is the possibility of at least two other women, plus his mama, who could bring drama and interference into the Man's life while he is trying to find his Wife.

Ladies, I would be cautious. Remember, we males are about the numbers of females. If he had one ex-wife, one baby-mama, one ex-girlfriend, and his Mother, then you, honey, would be at least number five on his list of females in his life.

PRE-HUSBAND SKILL #17 — PASSED ADULT AND CITIZEN MANHOOD TESTS

- A Man has passed the Adult and Citizen Manhood Test.

Ladies, if the male is 18 years old or older, and has not passed both tests, dump him immediately!

Males over 18 who do not possess a valid Man Card are not allowed to court or to socially interact with women. Talking with females is a privilege afforded only to Men holding their up-to-date Man Card. Business conversations between boys and women, such as: parents, teachers, elders, etc. are allowed.

NOTE: Until the infrastructure is in place to administer the Adult and Citizen Manhood Tests and issue Man Cards, give him ten points for question #17 on the test.

PRE-HUSBAND SKILL #18 — WELL MANNERED

- A Man is well mannered and polite.

Or does he constantly embarrass you with his stupid, immature, public behavior?

PRE-HUSBAND SKILL #19 — CONTROL FREAK

- A Man is never an egotistical, narcissistic control freak.
- A Man is a fair and effective family leader.

In nearly all human couples, the Man is the king and the Woman his queen. He is responsible for the welfare of the entire family, including providing shelter, food, clothing, transportation, and all the other necessities of an American middle-class lifestyle. The queen is in charge of the household. She oversees the family treasury, health and welfare of the children. She is also in charge of the family schedule, the honey-do task list, and the overall operation of the family household. The German word for this person is Hausmeister, literally translated it means "master of the house."

As Husband, the king must keep his queen happy at all times. As Father, the king is (chief executioner) primary disciplinarian to his sons and daughters. Extra discipline to the boys.

An aside here, I trust you, the reader, to reword these roles, as needed, to fit your modern day family. Yes, the career roles are shared and divided as the Woman and Man choose, both for their own self-satisfaction of their careers and for the financial safety of their family. For some, these king and queen roles are more crucial than for others. Nevertheless, I maintain that these roles exist and should be discussed and agreed upon between the Woman and Man.

A woman wants her Man to act like a Man. She wants her Man to be the king of the family as long as he understands his Woman is his queen. She sits on the throne right next to him. His leadership style as a Man, especially as a Husband and a Father, must tempered.

I use the analogy of "King" and "Queen." Being a military man, I prefer "General" and "Sergeant-Major." The Man is the "General" or "Family Commander." He maintains his coolness under fire. He goes forth and conquers for a living. Generals have to be the calming force on the battlefield, as well as with his family. For example, one day when Daddy comes home from a hard day of conquering, he steps in to a category 5 hurricane—wife and kids are screaming at 150 miles per hour. A Man, a Husband, a Father can get his family to a happy place within minutes.

The lady of the house, his Queen, his Wife is the Sergeant-Major of their home. Sergeant Major Mom, for example on a school morning, will push the kids off to school with minimal whining and quibbling. Because nobody disrespects Sergeant-Major Mom. Right?

If the Father is at home while Mother is at work. He will see to it that the kids get to school cooperatively. And he will insure when she gets home from a hard day, the household is in good order and is peaceful. The house is clean, dinner made, and homework being done.

PRE-HUSBAND SKILL #20 — SPIRITUALITY

- If religion and/or spirituality are important to the Man and Woman, they will figure out if it will enhance or interfere with their relationship and child rearing.

Are they close to the same viewpoint? By "viewpoint," I refer to how they will live as a married couple and eventually a family with children. Married couples from different religions can have healthy marriages. However, when the kids are born if there is a fight as to into which religion the kids are baptized, or inducted, nearly 40% of those couple divorce quickly.

I read about a practicing Roman Catholic man, and a practicing Jewish wife; the Husband and Wife did fine for three years. Each thought about converting to the other's faith but it did not happen. Once their first son was born the dad wanted him raised as a Catholic and the mom wanted him to be a Jew. Their marriage ended in divorce within a year after the child was born.

Men and women should work that out before the proposal because it could be a "show-stopper." Are you and he close to the same viewpoint on religion and spirituality?

MANHOOD BONUS TEST — PRE-HUSBAND, 3rd Ed.

This supplemental test is very different from all of the other Manhood tests. The test is administered by a single woman to validate if the Man she is testing could be a loving and faithful Husband to her. It will help her decide how to answer he should propose marriage.

NOTE: Once the infrastructure is in place the man being tested must have passed the adult and citizen tests beforehand, and possess a valid man card. No exceptions.

DIRECTIONS TO TEST ADMINISTRATOR:
1. Test is administered by a woman verifying if the Man she is testing will make a loving and faithful Husband.
2. This test may be administered with or without the Man being examined present.
3. Other women who have enough knowledge of the Man may administer this test. The more women who administer the test, the more the test's accuracy will increase.
4. Read to yourself all 20 questions.
5. Score each question 0 to 10 points.
6. Total the score (200 points maximum).
7. Use the scoring chart at the end of the test to determine the final results and the status of the tested male.

SCORING TIPS: You can score each question from zero (0) to a maximum of ten (10) points. When evaluating the question, consider whether the male you are testing has 100% succeeded on a particular question; that's 10 points. If he is nearly perfect, then that is an 8 or 9. If the guy is missing an important part of the skill, that is 3 to 7 points. If he is nearly failing, that is 1 or 2 points. And finally, if this guy you're testing is clueless on a skill, or just totally failing, that is ZERO points. Your objectivity comes into play.

The bottom line is your scoring will determine if this guy is husband material worth falling in love with ... or not. Be hard, be ruthless in your scoring. We cannot allow any male who is not ready to slip through.

Test him weekly, if necessary, to determine if he is scoring higher.

20 questions. 10 points each. 200 points total.

1. HAVE A JOB. Does he have a job? Does he have a clear career/life plan that maps out his goals as to where he is going in his life? Is marriage in his plan?
2. TRUE LOVE. Does he truly love you? Does he make you feel appreciated and respected for all you do for him? Does he make you happy?
3. COMMITTED RELATIONSHIP. Does he desire a committed relationship? Do you feel that you have picked your prince, the man with whom you wish to live for the rest of your life?
4. FATHERHOOD and CHILDREN. Does he want children? Is he, or does he want to be, a father? Does he possess the skills and aptitude necessary to be a patient and caring Father?
5. NEAT and CLEAN. Is he neat and clean: body, clothing, car, home, work, etc? Is he well groomed, organized, reliable, and punctual?
6. PERSONALITY. His overall personality: usually upbeat, humorous, rarely moody? He handles stress well and is a calming force in the relationship?
7. MONEY. He earns enough money to live decently? Does he manage his money and credit well? Does he have a financial plan?
8. SEX. Does he make it fun, satisfying, and stress-free? Does he manage his horniness very well? Does he have eyes only for you?
9. EDUCATION and INTELLIGENCE. Is he intelligent and educated enough? Or is he a stupid ignorant fool? Does he consider you to be intelligent, even smarter than he is? Or does he think you are stupid?
10. FRIENDSHIP. Can he be emotionally available to you? Are you his most trusted, best friend? Does he like people and does he like the company of others?
11. COMMUNICATION. Does he communicate well with you? Is he genuinely easy to talk to? Is he an effective listener? Does he take and give criticism well?
12. LOW MAINTENANCE. Is he low maintenance? Is it easy

for you to keep him happy? Does he enjoy life? Any mental disorders, issues or addictions?

13. COMMON INTERESTS. Do you and he share common interests? Does he share his interests with you so you can enjoy them if you choose to?

14. FAMILY and FRIENDS. Do his family and friends like and accept you? Do your family and friends like and accept him? His mom likes you? Your dad likes him?

15. GOOD CHARACTER. Is he a man of good character? Is he trustworthy, respectful, fair, caring, self-confident, and kind?

16. MOMMY and "EXs." Does he have any "mommy" or ex-girlfriend/wife issues? Any baby-mama, or children issues that interfere with the relationship?

17. PASSED ADULT and CITIZEN MANHOOD TESTS. Has he passed Manhood Tests #1 and #2 — Adult and Citizen? Does he possess a valid Man Card? **NOTE:** Until the infrastructure is in place to administer the Adult and Citizen Manhood Tests, give him ten points on the test.

18. WELL MANNERED. Is he well mannered and polite? Or does he constantly embarrass you with his stupid immature behavior?

19. CONTROL FREAK. Is he an egotistical, narcissistic, control freak? Can he be a good family leader?

20. SPIRITUALITY. Is religion/spirituality important in your life? Are you and he close to the same viewpoint on religion and spirituality?

SCORING, BONUS MANHOOD TEST — PRE-HUSBAND, 3rd Ed.

- **200 (100%) thru 190 (95%)—PASS.** He is a man! He is perfect! Marry him now! Say "I do" before your girlfriend with this checklist hooks him.

- **189 (94%) thru 180 (90%)—PASS.** Marry later! Needs only some polish. Ladies considering him for husband material should take more time with this guy before telling him she loves him. When he shines up to 95%, marry him.

- **170 (89%) thru 160 (80%)—FAIL.** Don't marry him! You could test him longer to see if he can score higher. But, he most likely will disappoint you. If he can't pick up enough points fairly quickly, don't screw around, dump him!

- **159 (79%) thru 140 (70%)—FAIL.** Dump him! Males who score in this range tend to be ignorant, whiny, couch potatoes, unemployed, living with parents, and lazy. Ladies, don't let him move in and don't loan him money. He's a loser who will take advantage of you.

- **139 (69%) thru 120 (60%)—FAIL.** Dump him immediately! He is an SOB and way too creepy. A psycho-stalker, mental defective, and a parasite who will steal your money, your car, and your heart.

- **119 (59%) thru 0 (0%)—FAIL.** Run away! He is a total bastard, ex-con, drug addict, dirt bag, etc. He is scary. Get a restraining order and buy a gun. Consider getting into the witness protection program.

* * * * *

Let's say the Man has passed Adult, Citizen, and Pre-Husband. Now he is fully qualified to get married, provided he has found his Woman.

They get engaged to be married. On this wedding day, the Man will take his 3rd Manhood Test — Husband.

CHAPTER 6

A LOVING AND FAITHFUL HUSBAND

Read that poem again. The author nailed it. Guys, read that poem a third time. It's like secret girl code, giving you a clue as to how a woman is hard-wired.

A Man makes his Wife feel genuinely loved and appreciated. He is faithful to her, giving her the satisfaction that she picked the right Man to marry. Remember the human reproductive mission: males want all females and females want the one, the very best male she can pick from the herd. Woman doubt their mate selection decision all the time. A Man will never allow his Wife to regret her decision to pick him to marry. I will say it again, because it's that significant; a Man makes his Wife feel genuinely loved and appreciated, every day. He is faithful to her, granting her the satisfaction that "saying yes" to his marriage proposal was the right decision.

This is the third of four duties of a Man. By the time a Man must prepare for marriage, he is already a mature and responsible Adult, a loyal and involved Citizen. On his wedding day, the Man begins his duty as a loving and faithful Husband. How does this Man get ready for his wedding day? Master the Husband skills. Some Husband skills overlap with Adult, Citizen, and Pre-Husband. Any duplicate skill also on the Adult skill list is "basic." If it's also on the Husband checklist, a Man has to master that particular skill at a more advanced level. Marriage in the developed world is dying. The great majority of Americans still say that they believe in marriage as a personal life goal. And they want their own marriage to last a lifetime. But their actual behavior diverges sharply from these stated beliefs. Marriage has declined primarily because we no longer value the institution as highly as we once did. Our culture has become increasingly skeptical of marriage, and of other institutions as well, that are thought to restrict or confine adult behavior. In their place, we now put a much higher value on individualism, choice, and unrestricted personal liberty. As a result, marriage has been losing its social purpose. Instead of serving as our primary institutional expression of commitment and obligation to others, especially children, marriage has increasingly been reduced to a vehicle—and a fragile vehicle at that—for the emotional fulfillment of adult partners. "Till death us do part" has been replaced by "as long as I am happy." Marriage is now less an institution that one belongs to and more an idea that we insist on bending to our own, quite individualistic, purposes. Fewer than 50% of Americans today include "being married" as part of their definition of family values. (COUNCIL)

Let me explain how I think marriage works. The components are:
1. The Committed Relationship
2. The Engagement and Wedding
3. The Marriage Contract

THE COMMITTED RELATIONSHIP. This element of the marriage is the "I love my wife and she loves me" part. It is the day-to-day relationship. A Man loves his Woman. He makes her happy by making her feel genuinely loved and appreciated. The committed relationship is the most critical part of a marriage, requiring the most attention from the Husband and Wife.

THE WEDDING. It's a pair bonding ceremony, a human ritual, and a big party all in one event. The wedding is the official ritual rite to publicly announce the couple and begin the marriage contract. It's where the vows are said. It is a big party and celebration of the new Husband and his Wife. In our culture, the wedding is centered around the bride. This event component of marriage is important for about a year before until the honeymoon is over. Then it's done. The Rite-of-Passage Husband ceremony is conducted on the wedding day while the bride is preparing. Only Men attend. When he walks out of the ceremony to wait for his bride at the altar, his is indeed her loving and faithful Husband to be. And he is ready and eager to marry his beautiful new bride.

THE MARRIAGE CONTRACT. Getting married is like forming a business, a partnership called the "Mr. and Mrs. Company." The new Husband and Wife sign the contract on the wedding day. The best man and maid of honor sign as witnesses to the marriage contract. Being married has many more advantages than disadvantages. Some advantages of marriage: married couples are healthier and live longer. A UCLA study found that people in generally excellent health were 88 percent more likely to die over the 8-year study period if they were single. Married couples get better tax breaks, higher credit scores, cheaper and better insurance. Legally, the couple has certain rights of inheritance, specific medical and legal rights not available to unmarried cohabitants. The marriage contract includes joint bank and credit card accounts. Living together does not work. Less money benefits than marriage. Couples who cohabit three, five, eleven, or more years, who even have kids and buy a house together, statistically experience a higher risk of separation than a married couple. The biggest disadvantage of marriage is the couple can't just split up and runaway. They will have to spend money to get a divorce.

Ominous Statistics:

- American divorce rate is 50% within in the first four years of marriage. Most of the time, it's the husband's fault.
- Wives file for divorce in approximately two-thirds of cases. (DIVORCE)
- The top five reasons for divorce are problems with: money, communication, family, sex, and addictions. (REASONS)
- Half of all husbands and wives cheat. (TUCKER-LADD) Males want more sex. Females want more love and appreciation. 20 years ago only 20% of wives cheated.

If she had used the Pre-Husband Test early on, the Woman would have dumped that cheating douche-bag before she fell in love with him. That test helps a Woman pick better Man. Since women now cheat as much as men, I will include a "Pre-Wife Test" to help men pick the right woman to marry. Women are not all sugar and spice princesses anymore.

SKILLS CHECKLIST — HUSBAND 2nd Ed.

1. Love
2. Faithfulness
3. Understands Marriage
4. Marriage Is Teamwork
5. Can Handle Money
6. Provider
7. Wife Is His Best Friend
8. Pamper Your Wife
9. Husband Character Traits
10. Leadership
11. Sex and Affection
12. Jealousy
13. Communication
14. Control
15. Protector
16. Values

Now the skills in detail. Followed by the test.

HUSBAND SKILL #1 — LOVE

- A Man—first and foremost—is a loving Husband.
- A Man understands and practices likability.

The foundation of a Man's relationship with his woman is love. He says "I love you" all the time: in person, by email, text, little love notes with the flowers and candy. A Man knows when his Wife is looking her best, and he says she is beautiful at exactly the right time. A Man tells his wife every day that he is the luckiest man in the world that she said "yes" when he proposed. He honors his Wife in public by making her feel like she is the only woman in his world and the center of his universe when they go out together.

I have been married for over 35 years. I still am not sure what love personally feels like for me, except to say that my life would be empty without my wife, Pat, in it. She is my partner and soul mate. I think that is how love feels for me. With that said, I am more focused on likability. It means being easy to like. I know my wife, Pat, loves me, but sometimes I am not sure she "likes" me. Love is essential, but I have to live day to day with a person who, at any given mood, may or may not like me very much. The Woman must practice likability. For a marriage vows to last, she must like her Husband most of the time.

HUSBAND SKILL #2 — FAITHFULNESS

- A Man, as a Husband, is loyal and devoted to his Wife.
- A Man has full control of his libido. He will never commit adultery.

A Husband is loyal to his Wife. A simple way to examine his loyalty is to observe how loyal he is to his family (i.e. parents, siblings, aunts and uncles, etc.). If the Man is loyal to the family he was born into, then he will be loyal to his Wife. If a Man's family he was born into is dysfunctional or non-existent, then he may keep his distance from them. And his relationship to his dysfunctional family may be forewarning as to his ability to be loyal to his Wife, and eventually his kids. Every Man is different.

My family is completely dysfunctional. The last five generations of the Lavelle family are scattered across the country, never communicating. My wife's relatives, the Ivies, are the polar opposite of my family. I have never met a more close knit and loving clan. They remind me of some of the kinship I observed in Asia and Africa. My wife's family are her best friends. They are a joy to be around. Every Man should have such a family.

A Man tells her every day how lucky he is that she said yes when he proposed. He makes her feel like a queen, his queen. A Husband never looks at other females for mating when he is with her. With his males buddies, or alone, it's normal to look at pretty girls, but no flirting, touching or any other inappropriate behavior.

A Man takes the time to judiciously select his ideal Woman to propose to. If a Man picks the right Woman to be his Wife, he will not be so quick to look at other females. His Wife makes a happy home for them both. In fact, she encourages him to bring his buddies to the house. She loves to feed them and let them play with her husband's toys, like video games. A Wife makes her Man happy. She willingly gives him regular loving, a big meal, and some new toys to play with. Oh, and an ice cold glass of beer to go with that sandwich, if he wants.

HUSBAND SKILL #3 — UNDERSTANDS MARRIAGE

- A Man lives by his vows.
- He understands the components of marriage: *The Committed Relationship, The Engagement and Wedding, and The Marriage Contract.*

He respects his marriage and knows that it flows linearly, passing through different stages over time. A Man treats his marriage as the most important part of his life, over career, friends, and his family. He must be a good provider and love his mother, but his Wife is his queen and soul mate.

HUSBAND SKILL #4 — MARRIAGE IS TEAMWORK

- A Man makes his marriage a partnership with his Wife.

Remember I said the marriage contract was like setting up a business? The couple are the owners and chief executive officers of the "Mr and Mrs. Company." Together, they work out their roles, the household responsibilities each will be responsible to the other for accomplishing. It is up to the Man to make sure the family duties are fairly distributed.

HUSBAND SKILL #5 — CAN HANDLE MONEY

- A Man ensures that he and his Wife are jointly responsible for managing the family finances. Together, they make the big money decisions.

In the Pre-Husband period, a woman should carefully observe how the male she is assessing handles his money. He must make that balance between proliferation (spending it all) and frugality (spending none of it). He never spends more than he can afford and he looks for value in what he buys.

- A Man keeps his family financially sound.

He would never put his family into dire straits with harmful debt. From the Adult skills, he has mastered the ability to manage money, and to use financial institutions like banks. He maintains good credit, paying all his bills on time. No matter who takes care of the family treasury, the Husband makes sure that his Wife is cared for and not deprived. He trusts his Wife's ability to manage the family treasury well.

HUSBAND SKILL #6 — PROVIDER

- A Man is an unfailing provider.

A Man is proud of being able to take care of his family. He is self-motivated, is ambitious, and has a clear plan on how to best provide for his family. Women want a Man who is a good provider. He should earn enough so that she does not have to work unless she wants to. Moreover, that money she earns is for her to spend, as she wants. Most likely, she will spend it on her family and her home. This is a mutual agreement made by the Wife and Husband together.

In today's two income households, do both the Wife and the Husband respectfully possess an equal say and an equal vote in the disbursement of the jointly earned funds? Is the agreement of who the provider is and who the stay at home parent is a mutually acceptable agreement?

A Man is hard working. A Man who works hard will impart that ethic on his children.

HUSBAND SKILL #7 — WIFE IS HIS BEST FRIEND

- A Man's Wife is his very best friend ... period. He can talk with her about anything.

It comes with the vows. She is number #1. The Man's brother, or father, or buddy is 2, 3, and 4. Nevertheless, she is always #1. First of all, communication between Husband and Wife is legally privileged. A Man should put his Wife first. However, there will be times when a man is upset about something; he does not have to bury it as we Men do. He can tell his wife. Wives will be more than glad to listen and care about her Man.

Women have big shoulders a Man can cry on when his mother dies or his favorite team loses the championship by one point in overtime. Women respect their Man for opening up to them about what is bothering him.

Your Wife is very loyal and trustworthy. She will always keep your secrets. A Man frequently tells his wife everything he likes about her. He can gently and respectfully let her know what he does not like because no one is perfect.

"A perfect woman, nobly planned, to warn, to comfort, and command; and yet a spirit still, and bright; with something of angelic light."
— William Wordsworth, English Poet

A Man genuinely cares about how his wife is feeling. He knows that, as a female, she processes life a little differently that he does. She may be delicate and sensitive. She may need to be cared for, or not. Some women are incredibly tough.

A Man gives his Wife space for her other relationships, such as her parents, friends, and colleagues. A Man would never stop his wife from hanging out with her friends sometimes, or engaging in her hobbies and interests outside the marriage, or wishing to spend time with her parents.

HUSBAND SKILL #8 — PAMPER YOUR WIFE

- A Man pampers his Wife.
- He regularly complements her that she is beautiful. Especially when she has changed her look or is wearing her hair differently or has a new outfit.

Send her to the spa for the full treatment. Do not make her feel guilty for spending money on makeup and nice clothes because a Man wants his Wife to look pretty. If she looks pretty, she feels good. And it makes her happy.

> "Women need three things—food, water, and complements."
> — Chris Rock, Comedian and Philosopher

He gives her gifts on all the important days: Wedding anniversary, her birthday, Valentine's Day, Christmas, and any other day designated as special. He also surprises her with little gifts at random times. Most women love thoughtful little gifts, cards, flowers, candy, etc. Gifts do not have to be expensive. The fact that her Husband took the time to get her a gift or write her a love note or card contributes to her feeling loved and appreciated by her Man.

- A Man makes time just for his wife.

Women love attention from their Man. Make conversation: share experiences, thoughts, and feelings in a positive manner. Being there for her; when she feels down, having you there can help her feel better. Be supportive, patient, and caring. Do activities.

Women enjoy physical time spent together doing stuff. Figure out what she likes to do that you can enjoy.

HUSBAND SKILL #9 — HUSBAND CHARACTER TRAITS

There are overlapping character traits with Adult and Pre-Husband. An Adult Man has mastered basic character traits. A Husband's skill must be more highly developed.

• A Husband must have an excellent self-Image.

If he has good self-esteem, he will not suffer from self-defeating behavior. I mean that a Man has a natural confidence and sense of self-worth. He is not narcissistic, arrogant or over-confident to the point of being reckless or negligent.

• A Husband is self-disciplined and goal oriented.

He uses his maturity and self-control to avoid temptation, such as adultery, drug addictions, etc. Self-control also keeps a Man from losing his temper.

• A Man respects his Wife's intelligence and capabilities.

He knows that his Wife wants to feel appreciated and respected. A Man is quick to apologize and atone for his mistakes without quibbling. He can be magnanimous, forgiving his Wife for her failings as well as atoning for his shortcomings and mistakes. He realizes that nobody is perfect.

• A Man is kind and gentle with his Wife.

Women often look for the inherent virile attributes of strength and courage in Men, to feel secure. Women select a Man who the Woman perceives as being the right amount of ostentatious, assertive, and a natural leader. A Man should stand up for himself. Sometimes he has to get loud and aggressive. However, by his nature he should be kindhearted and mellow. Martial arts is very useful to train a Man to balance his gender's aggressive nature with his amiability. A Man can be proud and humble.

- A Husband is reliable.

He is there for her when she needs him. He supports his Wife in all stages of life. He reassures her when she is not feeling her best. A Man never belittles or embarrasses his Wife intentionally. And he works hard to not do it accidently.

- A Man never disrespects his Wife.

He never looks at other women. He never fails to complete a promise he makes to his Wife. He never does anything to maliciously embarrass her.

HUSBAND SKILL #10 — LEADERSHIP

- A Husband is a skilled leader of the family.

An adult has mastered leadership and followership. As a husband, he must take it to the next step by being the leader of the family. Not a jerk. The family leader can adapt to life's changes. He is sensitive to how those changes affects his family and can "roll with it."

HUSBAND SKILL #11 — SEX and AFFECTION

- A Husband keeps his wife happy in bed.

He makes sex fun and stress-free. And he enjoys himself with her. He makes sure they can communicate about their sex so they can maximize each other's pleasure.

- A Husband is affectionate with his Wife.

He knows that women love attention and physical contact with their man. Not just the touch of sex, but hugs, kisses, hand holding, snuggling, petting, massages, even tickling. He has figured out what she likes. He kisses her to say hello and goodbye. He knows when to give her a big hug. And, of course, he loves to snuggle and to hold her hand in public.

HUSBAND SKILL #12 — JEALOUSY

• A Man has the self-confidence to not get jealous.

He is faithful to his Wife, and he trusts her to be faithful to him. A Man knows his Woman can handle herself like a married lady around other men. Moreover, she knows he will be there if she needs him to protect her.

Husbands do not bring emotional baggage into his marriage. He never disrespects his wife by comparing her to his mother, ex-girlfriends, ex-wives, or baby-mamas.

HUSBAND SKILL #13 — COMMUNICATION

• A Man masters the skill of interpersonal communication.

As a Husband, he communicates with his Wife completely. He is always open and honest with her, keeping her informed on everything. A Man makes time to talk to his Wife daily. He prevents distraction from inhibiting their communication.

• A Man masters the skill of effective listening.

He must refine that skill for communicating with his Wife. He knows she wants her Man to listen to her and to understand what is going on in her life. A husband understands that his Wife may only want her Husband to listen to her and not try to fix her problem. She may just want to talk it out and to sort out her own solution in the process. She may ask her husband for suggestions, and for his solutions. Regardless, he would never be so disrespectful as to ignore her nor to presume she wants him to fix her problems. He wants to know what she is feeling. A Husband understands that his Wife needs to verbalize her life. He listens and never tries to "manage" her.

A Husband can correct and not accuse those around him, especially children. As a Father, he is the trainer of his sons, readying them for Adulthood and Citizenship. A Husband tries to put his Wife in a good mood by making her laugh. He never resorts to physical or verbal abuse nor does he lose his temper. He is the calming force in the marriage. A Man can and does admit to his Wife when he is wrong and is willing to apologize.

A Husband embraces the famous quote from *The Hitchhiker's Guide to the Galaxy*:

> "I'd far rather be happy than right any day."
> — D. Adams, author

HUSBAND SKILL #14 — CONTROL

- A Man is not a control freak, with an obsessive need to micro-manage everything that is happening.

Controlling males tend to have a sense of inferiority that requires them to question loyalty and devotion. A confident Husband enjoys and appreciates living with a Wife who has strong opinions. She has a sense of self-worth, her own voice and individual life, her friends, career, hobbies, pursuits, etc.

- A Husband is not a narcissist who is willing to subvert his wife's needs for his own.

I would prefer the word "Command." A Husband must be the "Family General or Commander." To be a successful leader of the family, the Husband must have a "command presence": the exhibition of personal magnetism or charisma in a leader, the acquisition or development of which tends to promote an aura or mystique that encourages loyalty and discipline in others, making them more enthusiastic and effective, for the betterment of the entire unit and the success of its mission. (MIL TERMS C-CHARLIE)

> "Talent is more perspiration than inspiration."
> — Thomas Edison

I mentioned that if the Husband is the General of the family, then the Wife is the Sergeant-Major. The Sergeant-Major wears six big stripes on her arm. She gets her boots dirty as the master of the household, directly supervising the family and home. She requires the backing and team effort of the Husband to accomplish her mission of ensuring the household and its members are always in tip-top shape, ready to enjoy life and prosper together. The roles of the general and sergeant major are most critical once children are present.

HUSBAND SKILL #15 — PROTECTOR

- A Man makes his Wife feel safe.

A Woman needs to feel safe and secure, to feel that her Man will protect her from harm.

HUSBAND SKILL #16 — VALUES

- A Husband takes the lead in establishing sound family values.

He teams with his Wife to establish the ideals of their marriage and family towards which the members of their family have an effective regard. Values may be positive, such as the value of honesty, cleanliness, good communication, work ethic, and money management. And values may be negative, as being against cruelty, infidelity, or sloth (laziness).

MANHOOD TEST #3 — HUSBAND, 3rd Ed.

Once all the training is completed, the next step is to administer Manhood Test #3 — Husband. Since this is the third Manhood test, one would expect that, having passed three previous tests of Manhood, the Man being tested is fully prepared and ready to pass the Husband test.

The test is administered by the fiancé or wife, and at least two other adults who have intimate knowledge of the Man's training and preparation for becoming a Husband. The Man being assessed should be present in case a test administrator wishes to ask him any questions. A Man can be tested repeatedly until he can pass the examination.

Administer this test periodically starting when the Man is officially engaged to determine where his weak areas are for further training. The official test is administered before the wedding.
After the wedding, the Man should be tested at a minimum of every 2 years just to make sure he is fulfilling his duties as a loving and faithful Husband.

NOTE: Once the infrastructure is in place the man being tested must have passed the adult, citizen, and pre-husband tests beforehand, and possess a valid man card. No exceptions.

DIRECTIONS TO TEST ADMINISTRATOR:
1. Read all 16 questions.
2. Score each question 0 to 10 points.
3. Total the score (160 points maximum).
4. Use the scoring chart at the end of the test to determine the final results and the status of the tested male.

SCORING TIPS: You can score each question from zero (0) to a maximum of ten (10) points. When evaluating the question, consider whether the Man you are testing has 100% succeeded on a particular question; that's 10 points. If he is near perfect then that is an 8 or 9. If the Man is missing a important part of the skill, that is 3 to 7 points. If he is nearly failing, that is 1 or 2 points. And finally, if this Man you are testing is clueless on a skill, or just totally failing, that is ZERO points. Your objectivity comes into play. The bottom line is your scoring will determine if this Man is Husband material ... or not. Be hard, be ruthless in your scoring. We cannot allow any Man who is not ready to slip through.

16 multipart questions. 10 points each. 160 points total.

1. LOVE. Is the Man a loving Husband? Does he make his Wife feel genuinely loved and cared for? Does he regularly tell his Wife he loves her, and that she is beautiful? Does the Husband tell his Wife that he is the luckiest Man in the world that she is his Wife? Does the Man honor his Wife in public by making

her feel like she is the only woman in his world and the center of his universe? Does the Wife "like" her Husband?

2. FAITHFULNESS. Is the Husband faithful to his wife? Is he an adulterer? Does the Husband tell his Wife how lucky he is that she said yes when he proposed? Is the Husband flirtatious with other females, disrespecting his Wife? Is the Husband in full control of his libido?

3. UNDERSTANDS MARRIAGE. Does the husband put his marriage vows first? Does he respect his marriage? Does the Husband understand and accept that a marriage evolves and changes over time, passing through different stages? Does the Husband treat his marriage as the most important part of his life, over career, friends, and his family?

4. MARRIAGE IS TEAMWORK. Does the Husband make his marriage a real partnership with his Wife? Or does he treat her as a second class citizen? Or a slave?

5. CAN HANDLE MONEY. Does the Husband handle money well? Does he ensure his Wife is cared for and not deprived? Does he keep his family financially sound? Is there always enough money for the household to live comfortably on? Does the Husband strike a balance in spending, never frivolously spending their money, yet never being a tightwad? Does the Husband team with his Wife to jointly manage the family finances? Does the Husband insist that the Wife and the Husband make the big money decisions together? If the Wife is the primary money manager, does the Husband trust in her money management skills?

6. PROVIDER. Is the Husband able to properly provide for his family? Is he self-motivated, ambitious, and does he have a clear plan on how to best provide for his family? Does he earn enough money that his Wife does not have to work unless she wants to? When this is applicable, if she does work, does the Husband insist she use the money she earns as she wants, not just to pay household bills? In today's two income households, do both the Wife and the Husband respectfully possess an equal say and an equal vote in the disbursement of the jointly earned funds? Is the agreement of who the provider is and who the stay at home parent is a mutually acceptable agreement? Is the Husband a hard working Man?

7. WIFE IS HIS BEST FRIEND. Is the Husband his Wife's very

best friend? Does the Husband take full advantage of, have full appreciation of, and constantly learn from his wife's communication and empathy skills? Can the Husband tell his wife anything? Does the Husband trust his Wife to keep his secrets he shares with her? Does he enjoy talking to her about the "happenings of the day?" Does the Husband care about how his Wife is feeling? Does the Husband give his Wife space for the other relationships in her life, such as her parents, family, friends, and colleagues?

8. PAMPER YOUR WIFE. Does the Husband pamper his loving, hard working Wife? Does he regularly tell his wife that she is beautiful, especially when she has changed her look, or is wearing her hair differently, or has a new outfit? Does he make her feel guilty for spending money on makeup and nice clothes to look pretty for her Man? Does the Husband encourage his Wife to grow as an individual? Does he give her thoughtful gifts on all of the important days: wedding anniversary, her birthday, Valentine's Day, Christmas, and any other day designated as special? Does he give her little surprise gifts at other times? Does the Husband make special times for his wife to share experiences, thoughts, and feelings in a positive manner? Is he there for her when she feels down?

9. HUSBAND CHARACTER TRAITS. Does the Husband have confidence and a sense of self-worth? Does the Husband have positive self-esteem and self-image? Is he narcissistic, arrogant, or overly confident to the point of being reckless or negligent? Is the Husband self-disciplined and goal oriented? Does he use his maturity and self-discipline to avoid temptation, such as adultery, drug addictions, etc? Does he use his self-control to keep from losing his temper? Does the Husband respect his Wife's intelligence and capabilities? Does he know his wife wants to feel appreciated and respected by him? Is the Husband quick to apologize? Is he magnanimous, forgiving his Wife for her failings as well as atoning for his shortcomings and mistakes? Is the Husband kind and gentle with his Wife? Is the Husband loyal to his Wife? Is the Husband reliable?

10. LEADERSHIP. Is the Husband an effective family leader? Or is he a controlling jerk? Can the husband adapt to life's changes? Is he sensitive to how those changes affect his family and can he roll with it? Is the Husband fair?

11. SEX and AFFECTION. Does the Husband keep his wife happy in bed? Does he make sex fun and stress free? Does he enjoy himself with her? Does he make sure that they communicate about their love making so that they can maximize each other's pleasure? Is the Husband affectionate? Does he know that his Wife enjoys the non-sexual, physical contact of her Husband? Does he give her hugs and kisses? Does he hold her hand or take her arm when walking in public? Does he like to snuggle? Does the husband know what his wife enjoys in the bedroom?

12. JEALOUSY. Does the Husband get jealous? Is he faithful to his wife and trusts her to be faithful to him? Did the husband bring any emotional baggage into the marriage? Does he ever compare his wife to his mother, ex-girlfriends, ex-wives, or baby-mamas?

13. COMMUNICATION. Has the Husband mastered the Adult skill of interpersonal communication? Does he always share hassle-free communication with his Wife? Is he always open and honest with his Wife, keeping her informed on everything? Does he make time to talk with her daily? Does he prevent distractions from inhibiting their communication? Has he mastered the adult skill of effective listening and has he refined that skill for effectively communicating with his Wife? Does the Husband accept that his Wife may only want her Husband to listen to her and not try to fix her problem? Or does he jump right in disrespectfully and mettle? Does the Husband accept that his Wife, as a woman, sometimes needs to verbalize her life? Does he just listen or try to "manage" her?

14. CONTROL. Does the Husband have an obsessive need to be in control of everything that is happening? Does he enjoy and appreciate living with a Wife who has strong opinions? A wife who a sense of self-worth, and has her own individual life, friends, career, hobbies, and pursuits?

15. PROTECTOR. Does the Husband make his Wife feel safe and secure? Does she feel he will protect her from harm?

16. VALUES. Does the Husband team with his Wife to establish and maintain sound values for their marriage and family?

SCORING, MANHOOD TEST #3 — HUSBAND, 3rd Ed.

- **160 (100%) thru 152 (95%)—PASS.** He is the perfect Husband. The Wife should keep him and do all she can to keep him happy. If the Man is not yet engaged, then the woman who desires him had better get a ring on her finger fast before some other women hooks this Man.

- **151 (94%) thru 144 (90%)—PASS.** This Man is almost the perfect Husband, but, with a few rough spots, that should make him a "normal" dad.

- **143 (89%) thru 128 (80%)—FAIL.** This Male has enough issues that they distract him from being a good Husband. He may, or may not be salvageable. If he has passed the Adult, Citizen, and Pre-Husband tests, he may just need more training to pass this test. If he has flunked one or more of the first three tests, he is not Husband material yet. A woman should say "no" if he proposes.

- **127 (79%) thru 112 (70%)—FAIL.** Don't marry this Man. Dump him! Males who score in this range probably never took, or flunked, the Adult, Citizen and Pre-Husband tests. This Man needs to remain single and train hard to pass the test.

- **111 (69%) thru 96 (60%)—FAIL.** Dump him immediately! He should never have been allowed to take this test. He probably never passed the first three manhood tests.

- **95 (59%) thru 0 (0%)—FAIL.** Total bastard. Not a Man. Not a Citizen. Don't even think about falling in love with this SOB.

* * * * *

The Mission of a Husband is first to be an Adult and Citizen. Then to love and take care of his Wife. A Man should include in his personal mission statement that he wants to find joy in his life, and bring joy to others.

Now the Man, at this point in his life, has passed three of the four Manhood Tests: Adult, Citizen and Husband. He has found his bride and is ready to get married. The Man and his Wife should enjoy their wedding. And prosper in their marriage for a few years before making babies. Their plan should include deciding how many children to have and when to make them.

The final part of a Husband's mission is to master the skills of a patient and caring Father; prepare for the MANHOOD TEST #4 — Fatherhood.

CHAPTER 7

PATIENT AND CARING FATHER

"A truly rich man is one whose children run into his arms when his hands are empty. "
— *Author Unknown*

"It is much easier to become a father than to be one. "
— *Kent Nerburn, Author, 1994*

"Do not handicap your children by making their lives too easy. "
— *Robert Heinlein, Author*

Another excellent quote is "...easier to become a father than to be one." It takes a Man only eight seconds to impregnate his Wife. The Father will spend a lifetime caring for the results of those eight seconds.

I would say Fatherhood is the most challenging and gratifying duty of a Man. He has to bring to bear all the skills he has mastered as an Adult, Citizen, Husband, and Father. He mission is to prepare his children for Adulthood, and to find joy in being a Father as well as bring some joy to his Wife and kids.

Men are trained and tested to be Fathers, but we are far from perfect. We strive to fulfill our duties as Men and Fathers. Men accept that they cannot be a perfect parent at all times. He trains to be a good Father. When a Father makes a mistake, he will learn from his error and improve his skill. There are millions of Men out there handing their duties as a patient and caring Fathers. Embarrassingly, too many males are not. Here are some terrible and humiliating statistics compiled by the father's advocacy group InnocentDad.Org. (FATHER'S)

DISTURBING "FATHER" STATISTICS

1. **43% US children live without their father.**

2. **90% homeless and runaway children are from fatherless homes.**

3. **80% rapists motivated with displaced anger come from fatherless homes.**

4. **71% pregnant teenagers lack a father.**

5. **63% youth suicides are from fatherless homes.**

6. **85% children who exhibit behavioral disorders come from fatherless homes.**

7. **90% adolescent arsonists live with only their mother.**

8. **71% high school dropouts from fatherless homes.**

9. **75% adolescent patients in chemical abuse centers come from fatherless homes.**

10. **70% juveniles in state institutions have no father.**

11. **85% youths in prisons grew up in a fatherless home.**

12. **Fatherless boys are: twice as likely to drop out of high school and end up in jail; four times more likely to need help for emotional or behavioral problems.**

Social Media Comments to the question:
"What are the characteristics of a good dad?"

- "Be there for your kids. There is a difference between a father and a dad. A father is someone who just gave you some chromosomes. A dad is someone who raises you. He parents you. He lays down the line, but gives in sometimes. A good dad makes it a point to talk to his kids. It will help when they are teenagers and you want to know what is going on in their life. If you show that you care and trust them, they will feel more comfortable enough to come to you for things. Build a bond between you and them. Be a parent."

- "One who sticks around long enough to see your child off to college, or at least to high school. Mine did not stick around. Made my life hell."

- "Being a good father isn't something you can force. You have to love your kid unconditionally and be around when he or she needs you. It's not always easy, but it pays off in the end."

- "Protective, but not too protective. Loving, but not too loving. Caring, but not too caring."

This chapter will help answer the questions: how do Men become caring and patient Fathers to our children; how can a Man be the kind of Father his kids will love and respect; and what are the skills a Man and Husband must master to be that patient and caring Father who is loved and respected by his family? The answers are in this chapter.

SKILLS CHECKLIST — FATHER 3rd Ed.

1. Patience
2. Caring
3. Fun Dad
4. Disciplinarian
5. Time
6. Leadership
7. Teacher/Trainer

8. Parenting
9. Love
10. Protector
11. Father Character Traits
12. Communication
13. Responsibility
14. Reasonable Expectations
15. Not Mean
16. Wise with Money
17. Values

Now, the skills in detail. Followed by the test.

FATHER SKILL #1 — PATIENCE

*   A Man is patient. He has mastered the skill to accept or tolerate delay, trouble, or suffering without getting angry or upset.

Every Father can, and will, get angry with his wife and his kids. Every Man has a different temper threshold. A Father has mastered the skill of patience. He can keep his temper under control. When ambushed by a house in full chaos, Dad can put a smile on his face (even if the kids see flames shooting out Dad's ears).

I said that a Husband is the General, the "family commander." Generals are not allowed the luxury of getting emotional in a time of extreme stress by losing his temper and freaking out in front of his troops. Young soldiers can stress out in front of everyone, but the general cannot else he will lose his ability to lead.

A general must appear calm under fire, and in full control of his emotions, especially fear. On the battlefield, the general must instill patience and calm to help the troops control their fear.

In the family home, the Father too, must stay cool under fire, in full control of his emotions, especially fear and anger. He must always be the calming force to his family. The Father can only lose control in structured therapeutic places, like a gym, dojo, shooting range, meditation room, or buffet.

When the family storm has passed, he can sit down and talk to his Wife.

FATHER SKILL #2 — CARING

- A Man is caring, being kind and showing genuine interest in others.

He is always friendly and approachable. He is generous with his time for his children, and he is involved in what they do. He was a kid once. A Father wants the best for his children because he cares what kind of Adults and Citizens they will make. He wants to experience joy with his children and bring them joy.

FATHER SKILL #3 — FUN DAD

- A Man is a "fun dad" (as long as the kids are being good).

He has a funny bone. He maintains a positive sense of humor in performing his duties. A Man never loses his sense of humor. He doesn't take life so seriously all the time. He knows that sometimes you just have to run around and have fun.

Fun dads have better family morale than always-a-hard-ass Fathers do. Dads love to play with their kids. Dads have mastered the skill to act like a kid themselves. Dads are more interested in having the kind of fun that ends in a mess. Dads are funny and make their kids laugh all the time. They think their kids are the coolest people to have fun with. Fathers are responsible for initiating fun family trips. He creates family traditions.

FATHER SKILL #4 — DISCIPLINARIAN

- A Father is the chief family disciplinarian.
- He is never abusive to his family.

"There is a difference between a father and a dad.
A father is someone who just gave you some chromosomes.
A dad is someone who raises you."
— Anonymous

There is "Fun Dad," then there is "Father." The Father, as Family General, is in charge of carrying out punishments for family crimes committed by the kids. "Mom" is also cool. But "Mother," as the Family Sergeant Major, stands with Father on punishment day. Mother may unilaterally and spontaneously execute appropriate punishment on the children, but Father is still held accountable for proper enforcement of the family rules and policies, as well as managing the family discipline program. A Father loves his children. But, he has a duty to his children not to let them turn into spoiled brats.

There are too many parents who do nothing to stop their child's bad behavior. Self-discipline is a critical adult skill to master. Discipline is used the set boundaries. Kids are resilient. They will thrive and survive their childhood, continuing on to become responsible and mature Adults.

Pampering children is to indulge them with every attention, comfort, and kindness. It means to spoil. A Father pampers his wife, but not his kids. They get his love, his attention, and his caring. But, he will not spoil them, especially his sons, because he knows that a spoiled boy becomes dependent on others and will never become a Man.

"Don't handicap your children by making their lives too easy."
— Robert Heinlein, Author

The Father is the final disciplinary authority for his sons, and the Mother is for the daughters, especially when administering for corporal punishment. A Father has mastered the skill of administering discipline: the practice of training others to obey the rules or a code of behavior, using punishment to correct disobedience. As I said, the Father is the chief family disciplinarian. However, Father and Mother work together on the family discipline program so that punishments are fair and consistent for each child. A disciplinarian understands that each child is a unique individual with distinct personalities. Therefore, punishment for a family crime may be different for each child. A good disciplinarian has mastered all the punishment tools in his disciplinary toolbox (such as timeouts, isolation, verbal reprimands, and corporal punishment, etc.).

SPECIAL NOTE ABOUT CORPORAL PUNISHMENT:

Corporal punishment is physical punishment, the application of pain (such as spanking) to correct bad behavior. It is performed by an adult in authority over a child. And said adult is trained in the proper employment of corporal punishment.

In this politically charged society we live it, untrained adults may not want to administer corporal punishment because of the risk of abuse to the child and possible criminal charges to the adult. I am of the opinion that, if used correctly by a trained adult, corporal punishment is a useful and relevant tool to have in the punishment tool box. Especially for boys, as I know from my childhood experiences on the receiving end, pain can be a motivator to behave properly.

I said in chapter one that the baby boomers want to do away with corporal punishment because they believe that any use of pain to correct behavior does not work, and is nothing more than child abuse. Already, 23 countries have banned hitting kids; the United States is not one of them. However, in some jurisdictions, leaving even a small bruise or welt on a child from a spanking can cause that adult to be prosecuted for assault. Boomers cite studies that claim more than one-third of all parents who start out with relatively mild punishments end up crossing the line drawn by the state to define child abuse: hitting with an object, harsh and cruel hitting, and so on. Children, endowed with wonderful flexibility and ability to learn, typically adapt to punishment faster than parents can escalate it, which helps encourage a little hitting to lead to a lot of hitting. (BELKIN)

That reasoning is specifically why I advocate that all adults who will administer corporal punishment be trained first, before they can apply it. The training curriculum can be taught by child protective services, precisely defining when, where and how to use it. If the adult trained in its use stays within the training guidelines, then they are immune from prosecution. If a trained adult exceeds their training, or if the adult administers corporal punishment without the training, then they are subject to being arrested for assault.

Six years ago, the psychologist Elizabeth Thompson Gershoff, then at Columbia University, published a review of 62 years of research, analyzing 82 separate studies. And while there was a lot of evidence that spanking makes children do what they are told in the very short term, it seems only to teach children not to get caught. What it doesn't do is teach them to do better. (BELKIN)

I disagree. If used correctly, corporal punishment can and does teach children to do better. Of course corporal punishment will not work on every single kid. Another reason to justify the requirement that all adults be trained in how to use all the assorted disciplinary tools in the punishment toolbox.

As a little boy, my mom taught me to tie my shoes. I got pretty good it but, being a brat, I refused to do it. One day while getting ready for school, I whined to my mom that I could not tie my shoes, wanting her to tie them for me. She sat me on the sofa and said, "You know how to do it. Now I'm going into the kitchen. I will be back in five minutes. If your shoes are not tied when I get back, I am going to smack you, and it will hurt. I will smack you every 5 minutes after that until your shoes are tied."

I tied my shoes in less than a minute and still tie my own shoes to this day. The threat of pain taught me to do better.

Administering any type of punishment on a child is a skill that has to be mastered by all adults tasked with disciplining children. I cannot emphasize enough the importance that Fathers and Mothers be trained on administering corporal punishment before they are authorized to use it. As I said, corporal punishment is only one tool of many in a disciplinarian's toolbox. The training will teach adults that every kid is a little different. That one type of punishment might correct the behavior of one kid for the family crime. However, that same punishment, for exactly the same crime, may not be the best punishment for the other kids. Maybe one gets a spanking and one has to sit in the corner for a time out.

I was a product of corporal punishment in the 50s and 60s by the nuns and priests at Saint Peters Catholic school, and the principal of Crocker Elementary School. Not so much from my mom. I earned every smack with the ruler or the paddle. I was never hit out of anger nor was the pain inflicted abusively. I went on to my adult life with purpose. And had a good time. I was never maladjusted. I did avoid certain bad behavior because I did not want to get punished. Corporal punishment in American schools is still legal in 21 states. It works.

FATHER SKILL #5 — TIME

- A Man devotes lots of time to be with his children.
- A Father builds an emotional bond with his children, fully understanding each child's unique individual personality.

Dad knows how to have fun and has never lost his ability to act like a kid. Women complain that men still act like children. I argue that a well-trained Man has mastered the ability to enjoy acting like a kid from time to time. Adults do not play video games, kids do. So, Dad has to be a kid from time to time. It's how we men really have fun. That's why we still like toys no matter how old we get. For Christmas, Santa gave me an ice cream maker and a remote control helicopter. Thank you "Santa."

- A Man takes the time to listen and talk with his kids.
- A Father is approachable and easy to talk with.
- A Father is an effective listener with his children.

They will tell him everything if they trust him. If a Father is going to be the boss of the family, he needs to know what is going on. A Dad is skilled at developing his "confidential informants" among the kids.

A Father is all about school. Every school night he helps with homework, studying for tests, and completing projects. He has fun doing these with his kids. And he makes it fun for them. If the kids are having fun with their studies, they will learn more.

FATHER SKILL #6 — LEADERSHIP

- A Father is the leader of the family.

Mastering leadership is an Adult skill. It becomes more complex as a Husband, and unquestionably challenging as a Father. As I have said, the Father is the "family General." The success or failure of a Man's marriage is connected to his ability to lead as a loving and faithful Husband. More importantly, a Man's leadership skills determine the success or failure of a Father's children to pass the tests of Adulthood and Citizenship, to become mature and responsible Adults, and to live happy productive lives.

Total responsibility for the marriage and the quality of adults his children become, falls squarely on the shoulders of the Father. Family leadership is an incredibly demanding skill for any Man. It is so much easier to be a follower. It takes courage and strength to be a leader, responsible for the lives of others.

> "My father established our relationship
> when I was seven years old.
> He looked at me and said,
> "You know, I brought you in this world,
> and I can take you out.
> And it don't make no difference to me,
> I'll make another one look just like you."
> — Bill Cosby

I taught basic leadership in the military. The four basic types of leadership: *directing, coaching, delegating, and supportive.*

- **Directing** is when the Father points the finger in a direction, tells his family "we go that way." Everybody follows. This style is used only in combat, disasters, extreme crisis, and when the family is out of control.
- **Coaching** is teaching your children the adult and citizen skills, then taking them to the field and letting them practice, under the coach's supervision and mentoring, until the boys can pass the test. The coach helps with homework, teaches

driving, and supervises his sons performing their chores or other skills.

- **Delegating** is taking a day off from being the boss. He can ask Mother to be in command. Or his oldest child is in charge while Mom and Dad go on a date. Delegating can occur when Daddy just needs a break or he will become a crazy person.

- **Supportive.** The easiest type of leader to be is a supportive leader. That where Daddy sits in his chair with a remote in one hand and an adult beverage in the other. A Father can be a supportive type leader only when his family runs like a finely tuned Swiss watch. All is in order. Mommy and kids are happy and productive. The home is at peace. Daddy merely has to periodically say to his wife and kids, "Good job family, who's yo Daddy? You know he's proud of you and loves you very much. Keep up the good work."

- A Father is a role model to his family.

His good habits and bad habits are being watched by the kids. Children can oftentimes learn more about right and wrong from Daddy being bad than good. However, a Father is good at least 92% of the time or he loses his Man Card. Father can have one bad day about every three months.

- A Father sticks around.

Only a limp-membered coward would abandon his wife and children as 43% of American fathers have done. Those males bring disgrace and embarrassment to the 57% of fathers who correctly manage their fatherly duties every day.

A Father trusts his children, more so as they get closer to adulthood. He is not stupid. He knows his kids will test him. But, they know the punishment for the family crime of "lying to Father."

FATHER SKILL #7 — TEACHER/TRAINER

- A Man teaches his children. He trains his sons to master the skills of the Adult and Citizen Manhood Tests.

The Father is the prime source of knowledge in the ways of Manhood. A Father's number one priority is to prepare his sons to pass the Adult and Citizen Manhood tests by 18 years old.

Let me pause to address what some of you may be thinking; I have not forgotten the girls. There will eventually be "Womanhood Tests," but I want to first focus on the boys. They cause nearly all the grief in this world. Boys need a smack more often than girls do. Don't get me wrong, I know women are not all "sugar and spice princesses." A Mother's duty is to teach her daughter to pass the Adult Womanhood Test. Women, especially young adult women, are no longer trained to act like respectable ladies. They dress as nakedly as possible to attract the attention of males; they curse like sailors because they want to fit in and be cool." And probably the most reckless behavior of them all, girls and young women freely trade sex for male affection because they don't understand why they crave attention and affection from males. Girls have zero comprehension of the human reproductive mission. Yes ,our girls are failing. But, not nearly as badly as our boys are. I will come back to them after the boys are getting fixed.

When a Father spends time teaching his children from a young age onward, his children will learn to see the world through their Father's eyes. Sons learn how to appreciate and respect women. A Father will challenge his children to do their very best at home, in school, and in their lives. Trainer Dad expects mistakes and encourages self-improvement from them. A Father realizes his children are human and making mistakes are part of growing up. I said that before we oftentimes learn more from screwing up.

When he sees the children repeating the same mistakes over again or uncharacteristically making a lot of different mistakes in a short time period, the Father will have to use his leadership, interpersonal communications, and effective listening skills, and his patience, to find out what has gone wrong. And fix it. Kids make mistakes for different reasons, and not all of them for the wrong reasons.

A Father conducts family training exercises under the banner of fun. Like going on a road trip, or going camping, or building something. Or doing some community service. He even holds the family fire drill twice a year, just in case. He teaches his children to be self-motivated and have a healthy self-esteem, and confidence in their own merit as an individual person.

FATHER SKILL #8 — PARENTING

- A Man is a skilled parent.

A Father masters the skill of parenting, the process of training children to be mature and responsible Adults and loyal and involved Citizens. He is particularly responsible for ensuring his sons complete their training and rite-of passage, preparing them to pass the Adult Manhood Test.

Children do not come with an owner's manual. To master this skill a Father first must look to his parents, or lack of them. What was done right by his parents that the Father can use in his family? What was bad parenting by the Father's parents? None of that should come into his family. A Father never holds on to the parenting mistakes committed by his parents. All he will do is hurt his child and screw up their chances of becoming adults and citizens.

If there is more than one child, a Father avoids showing favoritism. A recent study found that parents do tend to favor one child over another for different reasons. (FOSTER)

A Father is aware of that phenomenon and will avoid it. He spreads his love, good humor, and leadership equally to the entire family. A Father is also aware of favoring his first child, often being the only child for many years, before the second child is born. The Father knows how to handle the changes that will happen. It will be up to Dad to make sure kid #1 still feels love and attention while the parents focus a lot of attention on the new baby, kid #2.

A Father as a parent is responsible for getting all the kids on one team with a clear mission. "Today, Kids, while Mommy is at the spa relaxing with her girlfriends, together we will clean the house spotless and make dinner."

A Father can admit his flaws so his kids will learn by example.

FATHER SKILL #9 — LOVE

- A Man loves his Wife and children deeply.

He will do anything for them. This is the greatest quality of a good Father. He loves his children when they succeed, and when they fail. We, as a nation, should better recognize on Father's Day, the millions of Fathers doing it right by their Wife and kids every day. Father's Day should be a national holiday. Maybe Congress passes a law to move Memorial Day to October and celebrate that holiday then instead of Columbus Day. Then Father's Day becomes a bona fide, federal, family holiday, celebrating Dad and the start of summer. What a wonderful idea.

A Father loves to show his affection in front of his family, showering them with hugs and kisses and "I love you." He encourages his family to do well, to be happy, and to find joy in life. His shares his love so openly that his family will feel loved and appreciated. He prepares his children for Adulthood, Citizenship, and marriage by teaching them how to love their country, their spouses, and their children.

A Father will make sure his children know he loves them and that he will be there for them, no matter what has happened. He likes to hang family photos on the walls to instill a sense of family, belonging and security.

FATHER SKILL #10 — PROTECTOR

- A Man protects his family from any harm.

When humans lived in caves, it was the Father and his sons who stood guard at the mouth of the cave, protecting the family from wild creatures and hostile humans. Fathers have a family security plan. He is responsible for the safety and security of the home and all members of his family, whether they are at home or away from it. Fathers are not perfect. They will sometimes act overly protective. And, many times, Mom can kick Daddy's butt when she has to. However, kids sometimes need their daddy to charge in, be the hero, and save the day.

A family learns that the Father is someone they can love and trust without the fear of pain or personal intrusion. A Father is the "go to" guy when things go wrong. It is expected that Fathers will be stern at times. But the family knows he is the person who is there anytime his family needs him.

FATHER SKILL #11 — FATHER CHARACTER TRAITS

- A Man will make his children see the value in everything they have.

A father loves to stimulate his children to new things, new ideas, and places. He gets a charge out of sharing with them the big, wide, wonderful world out there. He trains his children to appreciate things—their mother, their home, their school, their community, etc. He never lets his children take for granted what they have, from the food on the table to the nice clothes, and toys, that Daddy is paying for.

- A Father is open-minded, free from negatives bias, receptive to new ideas and change.

A good Father understands that times, people and tastes change over the years, and he does not try to maintain some inflexible standard of his own. He will go crazy if he does that. He allows his kids to be members of the society and the culture of their day and age. It is sort of a tradition that parents hate the music their children enjoy. Most boomers love classic rock, and hate hip-hop. Most teenagers and 20-somethings love hip-hop and maybe some classic rock.

- A Father is supportive and passionately loyal to his family.

Even though Dad may be an avid hunter, if his son does not share his love for the sport, or prefers ballet instead, Dad accepts it. A Father is his children's public defender, standing by them when needed.

FATHER SKILL #12 — COMMUNICATION

- A Father is an outstanding communicator with his children.

A Man has mastered interpersonal communication. He knows that there is a special communication between father and child. He listens to his children. A Father ensures his children feel that Dad is always interested.

FATHER SKILL #13 — RESPONSIBILITY

- A Father accepts full responsibility for the well-being and proper rearing of his children.

A Father accepts that he brought these tiny humans into the world. It is his responsibility to see that they fly out of the nest fully prepared to face the world as an Adult and a Citizen.

A Father who cannot, or will not, take care of his children should not be a Father. His Man Card is revoked.

FATHER SKILL #14 — REASONABLE EXPECTATIONS

- A Father has reasonable expectations for his children.

He is not unreasonable. His expectations are based on who they are as individuals. Fathers never try to achieve personal childhood goals that they could not accomplish during their childhood through their kids.

FATHER SKILL #15 — NOT MEAN

- A Father is not mean to his family.

He is a nice guy most of the time. Fathers can get cranky and moody. They have a lot on their plate. However, as I discussed previously, he is never, ever abusive or neglectful. And he is never a professional asshole (see Adult skill #40).

FATHER SKILL #16 — WISE WITH MONEY

- A Father is a wise, family money manager.

He teaches his children early on the Adult skill of money management, to prepare them to manage their own money.
A Man has mastered money management skills as an Adult. He earns enough money to take care of his family. He manages and budgets his money, working together with his Wife. Money is even more critical as a father. Kids are expensive. They like to eat every day.

FATHER SKILL #17 — VALUES

- A Father establishes sound family values to guide his children.

As he does as a Husband, the Father teams with his Wife to establish the ideals of their family towards which the members have an effective regard.

Values are those things, those ideas and philosophies each of us hold as important and fundamental in our lives. One of the duties of a Father is to teach his children right from wrong, and how to develop one's own individual moral compass. He values setting family standards, the family mission, and its goals. A Father values the rewards of hard work and of developing a work ethic.

MANHOOD TEST #4 — FATHER, 4th. Ed.

Once all the training is completed, the next step is to administer Manhood Test #4 — Father. Since this is the fourth Manhood test, one would expect that, having passed three previous tests of Manhood, the Man being tested is fully prepared and ready to pass the Father test.

The test is administered by the Wife and at least two other adults who have intimate knowledge of the Man's training and preparation for becoming a Father. The Man being assessed should be present in case a test administrator wishes to ask him any questions. A Man can be tested repeatedly until he can pass the examination.

This test should be first administered when the Husband and Wife are working on their plan for when, and how many, children to have. His official test is administered when his Wife has announced the pregnancy. After the birth, the Man should be tested at a minimum of every 2 years just to make sure he is fulfilling his duties as a patient and caring Father.

NOTE: Once the infrastructure is in place the man being tested must have passed the adult, citizen, pre-husband, and Husband tests beforehand, and possess a valid man card. No exceptions.

DIRECTIONS TO TEST ADMINISTRATOR:
1. Read all 17 questions.
2. Score each question 0 to 10 points.
3. Total the score (170 points maximum).
4. Use the scoring chart at the end of the test to determine the final results and the status of the tested male.

SCORING TIPS: You can score each question from zero (0) to a maximum of ten (10) points. When evaluating the question, consider whether the Man you are testing has 100% succeeded on a particular question; that's 10 points. If he is near perfect then that is an 8 or 9. If the Man is missing an important part of the skill, that is 3 to 7 points. If he is nearly failing, that is 1 or 2 points. And finally, if this Man you are testing is clueless on a skill, or just totally failing, that is ZERO points. Your objectivity comes into play. The bottom line is your scoring will determine if this Man is Father material ... or not. Be hard, be ruthless in your scoring. We cannot allow any Man who is not ready to slip through.

17 multipart questions. 10 points each. 170 points total.

1. PATIENCE. Has the Father mastered the skill of patience, to accept or tolerate delay, trouble, or suffering without getting angry or upset? Can he keep his temper under control? Can the father stay cool and collected under fire, in full control of his emotions? Is he the calming force for his family?
2. CARING. Is the Father kind and does he show genuine interest

in others? Is he friendly and approachable? Is he is generous with his time for his children?

3. FUN DAD. Is he—or will he be when his kids are born—a fun dad? Does he have a sense of humor? Or does he take life too seriously all the time? Does he like to sometimes just run around and have fun? Can he be called a "fun dad?" Does he love to play with his kids? Is the Father a funny guy who makes his kids laugh all the time? Does the Father believe his kids are the coolest people to have fun with? Does the Father initiate fun family trips? Does he establish family traditions, such as opening one present on Christmas Eve?

4. DISCIPLINARIAN. Is the Father a fair and effective disciplinarian? Is he the chief family disciplinarian? Does he work together with the Mother on the family discipline program so that punishments are issued fairly and consistently for each child? Does the Father accept that each child is a unique individual with a distinct personality, thus requiring that punishment for the same family crime may be different for each child? Has the Father mastered all the punishment tools in his disciplinary toolbox, such as time-outs, isolation, verbal reprimands, and corporal punishment? Is the Father the final disciplinary authority for his sons?

5. TIME. Does the Father devote lots of time to be with his children? Does he know that he is building an emotional bond with his children, absolutely comprehending each child's unique individual personality? Does the Father know how to have fun and has he not lost his ability to act like a kid? Does the Father take the time to listen and to talk with his kids? Is he approachable and easy to talk with?

6. LEADERSHIP. Does the Father accept that the skill of leadership is much more complex as the Father than as a Husband? That it can be unquestionably more challenging as a Father? Is the Father a good family leader? Is the Father the role model to his family, displaying his good and bad habits? Does the Father teach leadership, followership, mission focus, and teamwork to his children, especially to his sons so they can pass the Manhood Adult and Citizen Tests? Does the Father stick around or run away like a coward? Does the Father trust his children?

7. TEACHER/TRAINER. Does the Father train his sons to be

mature and responsible Adults? Does he prepare his sons to pass the Adult Manhood Test at 18 years old? Does he assist his Wife in training his daughters to be mature and responsible Adults? Does the Father challenge his children to do their very best at home, in school, and in their lives? Does the Father expect his children to make mistakes and does he encourage self-improvement within them? Does he teach his children to be self-motivated and to have a healthy self-esteem, confidence in their own merit as an individual person?

8. PARENTING. Has the Father mastered the skill of parenting, the process of preparing his children to be mature and responsible Adults, and loyal and involved Citizens? Is he responsible for his sons completing their rite-of-passage— from "boy" to "Man"—by preparing them to pass the Adult Manhood Test? Does the Father hold on to the parenting mistakes committed by his parents? Does the Father fully comprehend the dangers of favoritism, the preferring of one child over one or more of his other children? Does the Father avoid showing favoritism by spreading out his love, good humor, and leadership equally to the entire family? Can the Father admit his flaws so that his kids will learn by example?

9. LOVE. Does the Father make the family feel deeply loved? Will he do anything for his family? Does he love his children when they succeed, and when they fail? Does the Father show his affection in front of his family, showering them with hugs and kisses and "I love you?" Does he encourage his family to do well, to be happy, and to find joy in life? Does the Father share his love so openly that his whole family feels loved and appreciated? Does the Father ensure his children know he loves them and will be there for them no matter what happens?

10. PROTECTOR. Is the Father the family protector? Has he mastered the skill of family security? Does he take responsibility for the safety and security of the home and all members of his family, whether they are at home or away from it? Does the Father act unreasonably overly protective?

11. FATHER CHARACTER TRAITS. Does the Father love to stimulate his children to new things, new ideas, and new places? Does he get excited when sharing with his kids the big, wide, wonderful world out there? Does he train his children to appreciate their mother, their home, their school,

their community, etc? Does he ever let his children take what they have for granted? Is the Father open-minded, free from negatives bias, receptive to new ideas and to change? Does he allow his kids to be members of the society and the culture of their day and age? Is he supportive and passionately loyal to his family? Is the Father his children's public defender, standing by them when needed?

12. COMMUNICATION. Has the Father mastered the adult skill of interpersonal communication? Does the Father comprehend that there is a special communication between Father and child? Is the Father an outstanding communicator with his children? Does he listen to them? Does the Father ensure his children feel that Dad is always interested in them?

13. RESPONSIBILITY. Does the Father accept full responsibility for the well-being and proper rearing of his children?

14. REASONABLE EXPECTATIONS. Does the Father have reasonable expectations for his children based on who they are as individuals? Does the Father try to achieve his childhood goals which he could not accomplish during his own childhood through his kids?

15. NOT MEAN. Is the Father mean or cruel to his family? Is he is a nice guy most of the time? Is he ever abusive or neglectful?

16. WISE WITH MONEY. Is the Father wise with money? Does he earn enough money to take care of his family? Does he manage and budget his money, working together on this with his Wife? Is the Father a good, "family money" manager? Does he teach his children, early on, the adult skill of money management to prepare them to earn and manage their own money?

17. VALUES. Does the Father establish sound family values to guide his children? Does the Father teach his children right from wrong? And how to develop one's own individual moral compass? Doe he value setting family standards, the family mission, and its goals? Does he value the rewards of hard work and the developing of a work ethic?

SCORING, MANHOOD TEST #4 — FATHER, 4ᵗʰ Ed.

- **170 (100%) thru 161 (95%)—PASS.** This Man is "Father of the year." He is the perfect Father. The Wife will love being married to this man and making beautiful children with him. Ladies, if you are not married to this man, then you had better do it quickly.

- **160 (94%) thru 153 (90%)—PASS.** This man is more like "Father of the month" six months of the year. He is almost perfect but will growl at the kids sometimes, making him a "normal" Dad. If you have not married this man, again, do it quickly.

- **142 (89%) thru 136 (80%)—FAIL.** Maybe "Father of the month" once every couple of years. This male has enough issues that they distract him from being a good father. He has got about a 50%-50% chance of getting his act together to pass the Father Manhood Test. Don't even think about getting pregnant with him until he passes the test.

- **135 (79%) thru 119 (70%)—FAIL.** Don't make any babies with him. Dump him! Males who score in this range tend to be ignorant, unemployed, and lazy. He is a loser who will take advantage of you.

- **118 (69%) thru 102 (60%)—FAIL.** NO Babies. Dump him immediately!

- **101 (59%) thru 0 (0%)—FAIL.** Run away! He is a total bastard. As with the other tests, get a restraining order and buy a gun. If you made children with this loser, then consider getting the family into the witness protection program.

* * * * *

The Mission of a Father is first, to be an Adult, Citizen, and Husband. Then, to love and take care of his children. The Man has trained and studied for years. He has passed all four Manhood Tests: Adult, Citizen, Husband, and Father. He is doing well. He has a well-paying job. He is deeply in love with his beautiful Wife, and he is Father to wonderful children. More importantly, he has found joy in his life, and he brings joy to others.

What's next for the Man?

Now that he is handling his business, performing all his duties and responsibilities—as a mature and responsible Adult, a loyal and involved Citizen, a loving and faithful Husband, and a patient and caring Father—he is ready to join the National Elder Corps as an instructor.

I am still debating whether a Man becoming an Elder, should or should not, warrant another skill checklist, Manhood test, and a rite-of-passage. If so, I will add another chapter to the next edition of this book.

Until then, I would like to introduce in the next chapter, the rite-of-passage, as it connects to my solution.

CHAPTER 8

RITE-OF-PASSAGE

"We need the iron qualities that go with true manhood.
We need the positive virtues of resolution, of courage, of indomitable will,
of power to do without shrinking the rough work that must always be done."
— *Theodore Roosevelt*

How do we weld into a boy's skull that becoming a Man is the most important goal of his adolescence? All he lives for, more than anything else, is to become a Man? One word, training. Masai boys, that's all they dream about, the day they become Men. They know the ticket to the good life in the Masai culture starts when a boy becomes a Man, possessing those "iron qualities that go with true manhood."

Now, we arrive at the point in my Manhood program where all of the training is done, the boy passed the tests of Manhood. We honor them for their hard work of mastering the skills with a very special Manhood ceremony known as the Rite-of-Passage. The first rite ceremony is on a boy's 18th birthday, or when he finally passes Manhood Test #1 — Adult.

I believe I am the first anthropologist in modern history to publish any kind of Rite-of-Passage design.

Rite-of-Passage is a ceremony performed in some cultures at times when an individual changes his status, as at puberty and marriage; it is a "boy to Man" ritual. The Rite is hosted by Men, eventually by the Elders. Only Men may attend. It's a celebration and a party.

Nearly all Rite-of-Passage rituals have a "pain component" within the ceremony, with circumcision being the most common. The actual ceremony I envision has a pain component. The level of pain gets less with each test. The Rite-of Passage to Adult hurts the most.

There are four Rite-of-Passage ceremonies in a Man's life. The first, Adult, is on the boy's 18th birthday. This is the "boy to Man" part. The second is Citizen. That ritual is usually rolled into the "boy to Man" rite. The third, Husband, ceremony is held on the Man's wedding day. The fourth Rite is held on the day (or near the day) a Man's first child is born.

The Rite-of-Passage is in several common parts:

- *Pre-Game* (Before the event.)
- *Game Day* (The day of the event.)
- *Post-Game* (After the event.)

Rite-of-Passage General Requirements:

PRE-GAME
- Test Completed—Man being tested is present for questioning by the test administrators. There are usually three test proctors.
- Oral Interview—Man interviewed by test administrators.
- At the end of the oral interview the Man is authorized to get his Man tattoo. Added tattooing for each test passed.

GAME DAY
- Invocation
- Flag ceremony
- Host comments
- Man or Men introduced to audience

- Men show their tattoos
- Each Man makes a short speech thanking those Men who trained him and did not kill him instead.
- Men are awarded their Man Cards and Manhood Credential. For later rituals, their cards are endorsed for Husband and Father.
- Hugs and back slaps all around
- The Man Toast
- Benediction
- More cheering, applause, back slapping
- Buffet Line and Bar open after benediction
- The smoking lamp is lit.

POST-GAME
- Man Card briefing
- Duties briefing
- Next step briefing
- Report

All rites-of-passage ceremonies include all the general requirements listed above. What follows are the unique components specific to a particular ceremony, starting with the most important ritual of them all—Adult.

ADULT Rite-of-Passage Special Requirements:

PRE-GAME
- Biggest ritual of the four ceremonies.
- May need large room or hall.
- Location must accommodate buffet and bar.
- Plan on more than one boy participant. Up to 10 boys is a good number.
- Each new Man must read his career/life plan on Game Day. Make sure the boy did a good job. If a plan is thought to be weak, Men are allowed to throw things at the new Man reading his plan.
- Adult tattoo is the largest and most painful section of the four part Man tattoo. There are three more tattoo elements that make up the complete Man tattoo.
- Get tattoo done and healed to display on Game Day.

GAME DAY
- Should have guest speaker.
- This will be a drinking event. No attendees drive. Transport is prearranged by the host. All attendees drinking must have a Wing-man.
- Gifts are given: usually money, alcohol, guns, or cars.
- After the Man Toast, the Man removes his scrotum, lays it on the table, hits it with a hammer, hands the hammer to the host, who hits the Man's sack as hard as he can. Then the Man's Father whacks the sack, maybe a couple more invited Men whack the sack. The Man is not allowed to cry, yell, or scream. He must show great courage, concentration, and will power by remaining completely silent, still, and calm. When the hammering is completed, the Man picks up his sack, straps it back on, where it stays for the rest of his life.
- Use the special ceremonial hammer or mallet only.

I'm joking about the sack whacking. If you actually read that I was joking, then contact me with code word "Nuts." The tattoo is my pain component. Not everyone will read this far.

POST-GAME
- Lots of ice for the graduates.

CITIZEN Rite-of-Passage Special Requirements:

PRE-GAME
- Registers to vote. Bring proof on Game Day.
- Game usually held with Adult rite.
- Proof of at least 800 hours of community service is required.
- The Man gets the "Citizen" section of the Man tattoo.

GAME DAY
- American flag is on-site.
- New Citizen will lead the pledge of allegiance.
- New Citizen will sing the Star Spangled Banner a capella.

POST-GAME
- Votes at every election.

HUSBAND Rite-of-Passage-Special Requirements:

PRE-GAME
- Ceremony held at the Wedding location.
- Make sure the ritual is on the wedding schedule.
- Plan for 3 to 5 hours for the event.
- Arrange for food and beverages at the ritual location on Game Day.
- The Man gets the "Husband" section of the Man tattoo.

GAME DAY
- Rite is held while the bride is preparing on her wedding day.
- Bridal preparation time is 6 to 12 hours.
- The rite is hosted by the Best Man.
- Attended by all the groomsmen as well as all the Men attending the wedding: Fathers, uncles, brothers, cousins and male friends of the Bride and Groom.
- After the Man Toast, the Man being advanced to Husband, holds out his scrotum, his Best Man kneels down in front of the Groom and gently kisses the Groom's sack for failing at the tradition of talking the Groom out of getting married before his wedding day. After the kissing, the Man puts his sack away and heads for the altar.
- Event is done when Groom, Best Man, and groomsmen are called to the altar. All other Men who attended the ceremony return to their seats.

I was joking about the sack kissing. If you actually read that I was joking, then contact me with code word "Nuts." There is no need for the Best Man to try to talk the Groom out of getting married, because the Groom is a Man. And a Man always picks the perfect women to be his Wife.

POST-GAME
- Post Honeymoon celebration of new couple.
- With beer & honeymoon photos
- Carry-bride-over-threshold ceremony

FATHER Rite-of-Passage Special Requirements:

PRE-GAME
- This event can be held in a bar, someone's house, or at the hospital where the newborn baby is located.
- When the wife is pregnant, Game planning starts.
- Get good cigars.
- Appetizers, fast food, or snacks are the best food choice for this ritual.
- Man gets "Father" section of the Man tattoo.

GAME DAY
- The actual game day is the day the Father's first child is born.
- The ritual can be held as soon as possible after the delivery.
- No "sack" ritual as the Man will watch live, his Wife go through childbirth.
- Baby viewing.
- Father is awarded a whacking stick.
- Buffet and bar open
- Smoking lamp is lit for special cigars.

POST-GAME
- Send photos of new baby to all Men. Include all the birth info.
- Also send funniest "in labor" photo of Wife.

That's all for this chapter.

CHAPTER 9

CONCLUSION

"The greatest enemy of knowledge is not ignorance; it is the illusion of knowledge."
— *Stephen Hawking*

Tell the audience what you're going to say, say it; then tell them what you've said. "
— *Dale Carnegie*

I love those two quotes. Read them again. Hawking's I think talks about his dislike of Professional Assholes. I mention them in chapter 3 (Adult Skill #40). They are the only type of male human, of that personality type, who are very comfortable with possessing only "the illusion" of knowledge. They don't care that the rest of us see their ignorance. Being ignorant is how they get identified.

The Carnegie quote, I believe, was the inspiration for a saying I learned in Army Drill Sergeant School. Where I learned how to train new soldiers:

> *"Tell them what you're going to tell them.*
> *Tell them;*
> *Then tell them what you told them."*

Here is the "Tell them what you told them" part of the book. I confessed in the introduction that I am the worlds greatest writer. But I hope you got my message. And that you are as outraged as I am as to what is happening to our young men.

I wrote this book to save our boys. I want to help them become good Men. As an applied anthropologist, I found a terrible human problem infecting America and most of the western world. Furthermore, unlike many of my colleagues, I came up with a viable solution.

To recap, what is the problem and how did it get started?

STRAIGHTFORWARD PROBLEM DESCRIPTION: Boys are failing to become men at 18 years old. No clear definition of what it means to be a Man. How can a boy even reach Manhood?

We baby boomers originated the first strains of P-Syndrome, with our far-out and groovy (read lazy and anti-social) lifestyle. In a single, dope smoking, drop-out generation, we deformed the American national landscape, coercing a cultural paradigm shift in child rearing, transforming how we train our children to take their place in American society as successful and productive Adults.

We hippies ended 300 years of the Protestant Work Ethic and the "it takes a village to raise a child" social norm, replacing it with "only parents know how to teach their spoiled little bastards adulthood."

The present day consequence of the P-Syndrome infection is a generation of young American adults—who are failing in record numbers—to take their place as contributing members of our society. This is especially bad for the boys; their maturity rate over the last 40 years is plummeting. I asked your opinion in the introduction.

QUESTION: What percent of 18 year old boys are ready to:
1. Leave home
2. Take their place in society
3. As a mature, responsible Adult
4. With a clear action plan of how he will successfully and productively live his Adult life
5. Over the next 3 to 7 years?

I say 1 or 2 per 100 can do it.

In 1945, before World War 2 ended, nearly 100% of 18 to 21 year old males left home to join the military or work in the war industry. By the early 1960s, that number was about 80%. In 2002, it nose-dived to about 30% leaving the nest at 18. In 2011, my survey suggests an alarming trend, that the number is now less than 5%!

How do we save our boys and help them become Men?

STRAIGHTFORWARD SOLUTION DESCRIPTION: Define what a Man is. Lay out, in baby steps, how a boy can reach Manhood.

The resolution to the problem starts with you accepting that there is indeed a problem. Next, test all males 18 and older. We need to know how badly P-Syndrome has infected our boys.

My solution to save our boys is an eight step formula:
1. Acknowledge that the state of manhood in our culture is on the decline, and will continue to deteriorate unless we, as a nation, come together and fix it.
2. Clearly define what a Man is, and how a male can achieve Manhood.
3. Reset the legal age for males back to 21 years old.
4. Bring back the social norm of, "It takes a village to raise a child."
5. Ritualize Manhood training in our culture.
6. Post High School, Continue Uninterrupted Manhood Training.
7. Create a National Elder Corps Program.
8. Test all the males over 18 immediately!

Dear Reader, do you get it now? Do you understand what the problem is and what we have to do to fix it before America becomes a land of losers and cowards that no one in the world will respect? P-Syndrome is curable. Boys, read this book, learn the skills and pass the tests. It will take you several years to prepare to pass the Adult Manhood Test.

> "Pass the test.
> I will be proud to call you a man."
> – Jackie S.

When my plan is in place, first test all boys 18 and older to get our baseline. After that, we write the training curriculum, set up National Elder Corps, and start training our boys. Then, we test them again. If a boy passes the Adult Manhood Test, he is recognized as a Man, and warmly welcomed into the brotherhood of Men, at his Rite-of-Passage ceremony on his 18th birthday.

If we do nothing, by 2025, we will have elected a boy as our President. President Knucklehead will lead a bankrupt and weak, former super power, off the cliff unto oblivion. The world already looks at America as the pathetic nation of weaklings. I worry for my country that I defended as a soldier for over 25 years.

Historically, all great empires fail. P-Syndrome may hasten the demise of America before we have the opportunity to change the course of history.

I know some of you will question the validity of my work. Do not let your bias overshadow the core issue, what is happening to the American Man. P-Syndrome, the disease is destroying him and altering American society, transforming it from a proud and strong nation of men and winners to a weak and flaccid land of losers. How long before China replaces America as the #1 nation on Earth?

Now you know. Do something about it. Drop me a comment or two if you want at my personal email. Gallantry@lanset.com.

* * * * *

Epilogue

My nephew I talked about in chapter 1. The teenage boy with the king suite, two computers, internet, etc. Santa gave him a refrigerator for his room last Christmas. Since Christmas, he has experienced an epiphany causing him to now earn nearly straight "As" and keep his parents happy. He took the Manhood Test — Adult, at 16. He scored a 272 out of 400. Of course he failed, but he did earn a perfect score (10 points) on more questions than those he got a zero on. He gave away his video game system, saying he was too busy with school. He is on his way to becoming an adult on time. I have hope for the boy.

The other story, that young male named Rick whom I mentioned in chapter 1. Today, 31 March 2012, he finally landed a job with decent pay and benefits. His father spent every day of the last two months transporting his 26 year old son all over town to apply for jobs, attend job fairs, and make it to interview appointments. I salute the Father for doing what he needed to do help his son. Now, we can only wait and hope the boy does not screw it up and get fired as he did from previous jobs.

Appendixes

This is a simple chart of a Man's life, from birth to retirement. Age is the key. At a certain age the male undergoes the various manhood tests, rite of passage ceremonies.

AGE	RANK	ACTION/EVENT	COMMENTS
		Appendix #1, Man Life Chart	
0	Child	Born	
0-5	Child	Preschool	• Have fun but learn to be a good baby. • Preschool learn to socialize and elementary character development • Team building
6-12	Adolescent/Boy/Student	Start Adult Skills Checklist	• Training begins at home and in school. • Elders are now involved. • May see some newly minted Men assisting Elders • Work on the first 10 to 20 skills
13-17	Adolescent/Boy/Student	• Finish Adult Basic skills • Manhood test #1—Adult (pretest) • Start on citizen skill checklist • Start on pre-husband skill checklist	• To get ahead of the process, he should master all the skills by 17. He must master them by 18. • Take a practice test to determine what needs work before final adult test • Passes the adult test he in now designated a man. At 18 he can participate in Rite of Passage Ceremony #1 and be official ordained a Man. • First Right-Of Passage Ceremony to formally announce that this boy is now a man. And is to be treated with respect due his status. • But he is still a young adult. • Must learn how to properly practice courtship.
18	MAN/Adult (Novice)/Adolescent	• Pass Manhood Test #1—Adult • Rite of Passage Ceremony #1 • Citizen skills practice & field work • Continue working on Pre-husband skills	• A a novice must continue to refine his adult skills. • In the Masai culture he would be called a "junior warrior."
20	MAN/Adult (Novice)/Adolescent	• Manhood test #2 – Citizen (pretest) • Retake Manhood Test #1—Adult to validate still qualified as adult • Continue working on Pre-husband skills	

Age	Category		
21	MAN/Adult/Citizen/ Adolescent	• Pass Manhood Test #2—Citizen • Passes test #1 & #2, then proceed to Rite of Passage ceremony #2 • Take Manhood Bonus Test —Pre-husband	• Rite of Passage ceremony #2 is to announce to this man is no longer a Novice, but a full-fledged adult and citizen. • Continue working on Pre-husband skills • Become assistant trainer to work with elders in teaching the younger boys. • Should be able to pass Manhood Bonus Test— Pre-husband.
21-26	MAN/Adult/Citizen/ Adolescent	• Pass Manhood Bonus Test —Pre- husband • Improve cash flow • Find wife	
23-29	MAN/Adult/Citizen/ Adolescent	• Have really good job • Buy House • Find Wife • Get Engaged • Start mastering Husband Skills checklist	• Men get to wear an engagement ring also.
26-32	MAN/Adult/Citizen/ Husband	• Manhood test #4—Husband (Pretest) • Get Married • Rite of Passage Ceremony #3—Wedding • Start mastering Father Skills Checklist • Elder Training	• In the Masai culture the man would now be designated a senior warrior. • Wedding are to be made as special for the Man as it is for the women
27-35	MAN/Adult/Citizen/Husband/Father	• First Child Born • Rite of Passage Ceremony #4—First Born • Manhood Test #5—Father (Pretest) • Elder Training	• A man should have already been getting prepared for the father test.
28-36		• Pass Manhood Test #5—Father	
36-50		• Graduate from Elder Training • Rite of Passage Ceremony #5—Elder	• Become a certified Elder • In Masai Culture the man would be designated a junior elder
62-70		• Retire	• Can continue Elder duties under no longer able to.

APPENDIX 2: SKILLS CHECKLIST — ADULT, 3rd Ed.

1. Bathing
2. Oral Care
3. Dressing
4. Grooming
5. Using a toilet
6. Eating/Feeding Yourself
7. Shopping
8. Cooking
9. General Cleaning and Chores
10. Laundry
11. Character Development
12. Organization
13. Punctuality
14. Health Management
15. Effective Interpersonal Communication
16. Etiquette, Manners
17. Proficient Student
18. Goal Setting
19. Citizenship
20. Driving
21. Courtship and Girls
22. Proper Use of Communication Methods
23. Managing Finances
24. Life/Career Planning
25. Pet/Animal Care
26. Work
27. Spirituality
28. Find A Place to Live
29. Quibbling
30. Stress and Anger Management
31. Property Management—Personal and Common Items
32. Borrowing and Loaning
33. Libido Management
34. Time Management
35. Teamwork
36. Good Decision Making
37. Followership and Leadership
38. Relationship Management

39. A Moral Compass
40. Don't Become a Professional Asshole

APPENDIX 3: MANHOOD TEST #1 — ADULT, 5th Ed.

If you have any suggestions to make this and any other test a more effective tool, please email me personally, gallantry@lanset.com.

Once all the training is completed, the last step to adulthood is to administer the first test of manhood: Manhood Test #1 — Adult. Pass the test and a boy is an adult and a man. Fail and he remains a boy in remedial training until he can be tested again.

The test is administered by a minimum of three adults, who have intimate knowledge of the boy's training and preparation for adulthood. Test administrators should include a combination of parents, teachers, clergy, or Elders. The boy being assessed should be present in case a test administrator wishes to ask the boy any questions.

Administer this test periodically before the boy turns 18 to determine what his weak areas are for further training. The official test is taken between 17 ½ and 18 ½ years old. If he fails at 18 ½, he must participate in remedial training. A boy can be tested repeatedly until he can pass the examination. Once he has been deemed ready to take the test again, the entire examination will be repeated.

DIRECTIONS TO TEST ADMINISTRATOR:
1. Read all 40 questions.
2. Score each question 0 to 10 points.
3. Total the score (400 points maximum).
4. Use the scoring chart at the end of the test to determine pass or fail and the status of the tested boy.

SCORING TIPS: You can score each question from zero (0) to a maximum of ten (10) points. When evaluating the question, consider whether the male you are testing has 100% succeeded on a particular question; that's 10 points. If he is near perfect, then that is an 8 or 9. If the guy is missing a important part of the skill, that is a 3 to a 7. If he is nearly failing, that is 1 or 2 points. And finally, if this guy you're testing is clueless on a skill, or just totally failing, that is ZERO points. Your subjectivity comes into play. The bottom line is your scoring will determine if this guys is an Adult and a Man ... or not. Be hard, be ruthless in your scoring. We cannot allow any male who is not ready to slip through.

Consider mastering the Adult skills and passing the first Manhood Test as a rite-of-passage. If you pass a boy, and he fails to perform as an adult, you may have to explain why you passed him. Remember the Heinlein quote, "Never handicap your children by making their lives too easy." This test must take years to prepare for and be tough to pass. Remember, no matter how hard we train and mentor and prepare our boys for the test, some guys were just never meant to be adults. A certain percentage will be chronic failures for a variety of reasons.

40 multipart questions. 10 points each.
400 points total.

1. BATHING. Does he wash every day, using a clean wash rag, a scrub brush, and lots of soap and hot water? Does he use a clean towel to dry, not a dirty rag that's been on the floor for 6 months? He washes his hair with shampoo? Does he wear fresh clean underwear and socks every day?
2. ORAL CARE. Does he brush and floss teeth daily after every meal, or at least once per day before bedtime? Does he use mouthwash and breath mints?
3. DRESSING YOURSELF. Is he able to select appropriate clothing for the situation? Is he able to dress himself in clean, neat, well-maintained clothes and shoes? Does he know what to wear for a given function, like going to work or school?
4. GROOMING. Does he regularly shave, get a haircut, comb his hair, clean and trim his fingernails and toenails? Does he carry a clean handkerchief to blow his nose? Does he keep his fingers out of his nose? Does he spit in public?
5. USING A TOILET. Does he put the "brown" in the toilet, not on the floor or in his pants? Does he put the "yellow" in the bowl or urinal, not on the floor, walls, or in the hamper? Does he ALWAYS flush when finished? Does he thoroughly wipe?

Does he wash his hands every time after using the toilet?

6. EATING/FEEDING/TABLE MANNERS. Does he eat politely, with good table manners? Does he use a knife, fork, spoon, or chopsticks to eat, and not his fingers, unless it is a sandwich or fried chicken? Does he use a napkin, not his sleeve or table cloth? Does he chew his food with his mouth open, or stuff his face with so much food he looks like a chipmunk storing nuts for the winter? Does he make animal noises while he chews? Does he talk with food in his mouth? Does he reach over others at the table for food? Does he take food away from others without asking permission? Does he stuff himself until he can't breathe?

7. SHOPPING. Is he able to shop for everything needed to live an Adult life in the 21st century? Can he make a shopping list, know where to buy the items, and how to pay for them? Does he know what things cost and how to shop for the best value? Does he do errands for himself and others? Does he buy gifts, especially for the women in his life: his mom, sister, wife, and girlfriend?

8. COOKING/MEAL PREPARATION. Can he buy food? Can he cook fresh food as well as heat up pre-made meals? Can he read and follow recipes? Can he use a stove, oven, microwave oven, and basic kitchen equipment? Can he set a table? Is he able to menu plan and prepare balanced nutritious dishes for breakfast, lunch, dinner, and snacks? After each meal is prepared, does he clean the kitchen (or BBQ) and do the dishes, etc?

9. HOUSEWORK/CHORES/CLEANING. Does he do chores? Does he keep his living and sleeping area spotless? Does he clean all rooms in the house, especially the bathroom and kitchen? Can he clean anything in the home: work/study area, garage, yards and garden, cars, dog, etc? Does he know how to use the correct cleaning products and equipment for a specific cleaning job?

10. LAUNDRY. Does he wash and iron his own clothes? Does he sort his own clothes? Does he know how to use a washer, dryer, and iron? Does he know which laundry products to use and when? Can he use a dry cleaners?

11. CHARACTER DEVELOPMENT. Does he possess the positive character traits of: trustworthiness, respect, responsibility,

fairness, caring, citizenship, patience, kindness, generosity, and loyalty?

12. ORGANIZATION. Does he manage all the parts of his life? Is he organized; does he keep track of his daily schedule, like classes, work, appointments, dates, interviews, due dates for homework, bills, filing taxes, cashing in winning lottery tickets, etc? Does he possess a calendar/appointment book? Does he read and update it every morning or before going to bed? Does he keep files for his receipts and legal documents like auto sales contracts, sales/repair agreements, car registration copies, insurance policies, warranties, leases, etc? Does he, at all times, carry a pen and something to write on? Can he read and understand basic legal documents, including: simple contracts, insurance and medical forms, sales documents, loan and credit contracts, leases and rental agreements, etc?

13. PUNCTUALITY. Does he get there on time, a little early even? Does he use that written schedule to be on time for work, classes, appointments, interviews, etc? Is he on time for when stuff like homework and bills are due and for dates with a girlfriend, etc? Does he carry a time piece at all times? Does he, on the rare occasion when he will be late, call to let them know he will be late? Can he use a map and/or GPS?

14. HEALTH MANAGEMENT. Does he take care of his health: his physical health, dental health, and mental health? Does he get an annual physical and dental exam? Does he get his teeth cleaned at least once a year? If required, does he take his medication as prescribed? Can he refill his prescriptions? Does he know how to use over-the-counter medication like aspirin? Can he care for himself if he gets a cold, headache, or is hung over? Is he trained in First Aid, CPR, and how to use the newest Automated External Defibrillators that are in most workplaces, schools, and some homes? Does he manage his health care insurance?

15. INTERPERSONAL COMMUNICATION. Can he communicate on different interpersonal levels depending upon with whom he is communicating? Is he careful with his communication or does he have a "big mouth?" Is he an effective listener? Does he speak and write with proper grammar, vocabulary, and pronunciation? Does he practice not saying anything too stupid? Does he write neatly and literately?

16. ETIQUETTE and GOOD MANNERS. Does he behave when in front of polite company? Is he courteous and respectful, especially, when communicating to parents, grandparents, teachers, and all Adults? Does he use "Sir" when talking to a Man, and "Ma'am" when addressing a Woman? Can he shake hands and greet people properly? Does he use profanity in public? Does he greet everyone he meets or passes on the street with a "good morning," or "good afternoon," or some other simple acknowledgement of that other person's presence? Does he, when passing another Man, make brief eye contact, acknowledge the contact with a simple greeting or a head nod of recognition?

17. PROFICIENT STUDENT. Is he an excellent student? Does he always study hard and perform well in his training and education? Is he a polite and respectful student? Does he stay out of trouble at school? Does he know how to prepare for school, how to enroll in college or trade school, and what is required to graduate? If he is going to college, will his education lead to a well-paying job?

18. GOAL SETTING. Does he set, for himself, short, medium, and long term goals? Does he write them down? Does he usually accomplish his goals?

19. CITIZENSHIP. Is he a loyal and involved citizen? Does he obey the law? Is he a good neighbor? Does he understand how government works? Does he know who his elected representatives are? Does he perform community service in some form? Did he register to vote on his 18th birthday?

20. DRIVING/DRIVER LICENSE/TRANSPORTATION. Does he have a valid driver's license to operate any standard passenger automobile? Is he a safe and courteous driver? Has he purchased a personal vehicle? Does he keep his vehicle in good mechanical condition? Does he keep his vehicle clean? Does he make all his of vehicle payments on time? Does he have proof of vehicle insurance? Does he keep his vehicle validly registered? Can he use any form of public transportation? Can he travel by air or rail, including planning the travel, scheduling, and purchasing tickets? Does he ride and take care of a bike?

21. GIRLS AND COURTSHIP. Is he clear as to his courtship mission: to find the perfect woman to be his Wife; and mother

of his children? Does he know how to be polite and charming, making the women around him feel comfortable and secure? Can he properly court and woo a woman? Does he know how to approach and meet females? How to make them happy? Does he know what qualities he wants in a wife? Has he learned all he can about women: how they think; their behavior patterns; and why they act the way they do? Does he understand the fundamental steps of courtship? Does he understand the species Homo Sapiens' mating biology? Does he understand his biological mating mission and hers?

22. USING COMMUNICATION DEVICES. Does he properly and courteously use all electronic communication methods and devices: telephones, internet, email, texting, and, of course, social media? Does he communicate properly using any device he has mastered? Is he literate; able to speak, read, and write English with enough skill that he is understood and he can understand others who speak English? Does he use good manners while communicating, and is courteous and respectful? Does he know how to type on all keyboards he uses? Is he respectful of others by not disturbing them while using a communication device? Does he realize there is no privacy in cyberspace? He is careful as to what communication he puts out there? Can he obtain a cell phone, get high speed internet, buy and use a computer? He can email and text?

23. MANAGING FINANCES. Does he know how to make money? Does he manage his money? Does he have a financial plan? Does he use and properly manage his bank accounts? His ATM/Debit card? His credit card? Does he pay off his credit card balance every month? Does he balance and reconcile all bank accounts monthly? Can he start and manage an investment/retirement account? Does he use computer software to manage his personal finances? Does he prepare and file his own federal and state tax returns? Can he submit scholarship and student loan paperwork? Does he understand basic economics: stock markets, Federal Reserve, GDP, inflation, banking, marketplace, deficit spending, etc? Does he maintain good credit and FICO score? Does he maintain proper cash flow? Does he pay all his bills on time?

24. PET/ANIMAL OWNERSHIP AND CARE. Does he take care of all animals he is responsible for, every day? Does he assess

the number and types of pets he can responsibly manage? Does he enjoy all the animals in his care?

25. WORK/FIND A JOB. Does he have a work ethic? Can he always find a paying job, in an environment that pays well, and that he enjoys? Does he figure out what job he wants, networks it, trains for it, then applies, interviews, and gets hired? Does he know how to keep a job? Is he a reliable worker?

26. FIND A PLACE TO LIVE. Does he accurately calculate his cost of living budget? Does he locate suitable housing on or under his budget? Does he complete all lease/rental agreements? Does he obtain and maintain renters insurance? Does he keep his home clean and in good order? Does he obtain utilities, including internet, cable/satellite TV, gas, electric, etc? Does he maintain a professional relationship with his landlord and his neighbors? Does he know how to buy a house?

27. LIFE/CAREER PLANNING. Does he have a life career plan? Does he know where he is going in life, at least in the first 4 to 7 years?

28. SPIRITUALITY. Does he have some spirituality in him? Has he found something to fill his spiritual needs?

29. QUIBBLING. Does he whine or quibble? Does he make excuses for his failures?

30. STRESS and ANGER MANAGEMENT. Does he stay cool and calm when it hits the fan? Does he control his anger? Is he patient and able to bring calmness, not add stress? Does he use stress relievers like boxing, martial arts or meditation?

31. BORROWING and LOANING. When he borrows someone else's property, does he always return it on time in the same condition (or better) than when he got it? If he loses or damages other person's property, does he quickly offer an apology and pay for a replacement or repair? Does he loan his property only to other Men, not to a boy unless properly supervised? If he loans money, is he clear on the terms, payment due dates and amount? Or does he make it clear to the borrower that he intends to give that money away as a gift with no expectation of payback?

32. PROPERTY MANAGEMENT. Does he respect and take care of his personal property (from clothes to a car to a house) and the property of others he is responsible for? Does he keep track of his property, keep it in good working order and replace it as

needed? Does he minimize hoarding and pack ratting?

33. LIBIDO MANAGEMENT. Does he manage his libido? Does he practice certain techniques that enable him to keep his libido under control?

34. TIME MANAGEMENT. Does he organize his time so he can get done what needs doing, and maybe have some spare time to enjoy life? Does he use a written schedule and some type of clock to track time, to not miss appointments?

35. TEAMWORK. Is he a loyal team member and competent team leader? Does he join some type of team: sports, scouts, recreational, military, work, etc? Does he put the needs of his teammates before his own needs? Is he mission-focused?

36. GOOD DECISION MAKING. Does he make good decisions ... most of the time? Does he have good judgment and common sense; have that ability to make a decision objectively, authoritatively, and wisely, especially in serious or consequential matters? Does he usually make some decision, good or bad, rather than none at all? Does he practice making good decisions under various situations and time constraints?

37. RELATIONSHIP MANAGEMENT. Does he consider all of his relationships to be important and worthy of his time? Does he cultivate and maintain his relationships? Is his personal philosophy to give more of himself and to expect less from others in maintaining and managing healthy relationships? Does he stay in touch?

38. A MORAL COMPASS. Does he have a moral compass? Does he clearly know the difference between wrong and wrong, good and bad?

39. LEADERSHIP and FOLLOWERSHIP. Is he an effective and competent leader, who can build and lead a cohesive team? Is he a loyal "follower" and team member, one who can be counted on do his part to accomplish the team's mission? Is he ever a "control freak" or an incompetent leader?

40. PROFESSIONAL ASSHOLE. Is he a "Professional Asshole?" Is he, on the rare occasion when he must be, an amateur asshole until what needs doing is done? Then, does he revert back to his normal courteous, kind and caring demeanor? Does he understand the different types of assholes, "Professional vs. Amateur?"

SCORING,
MANHOOD TEST #1 — ADULT, 5th Ed.

- **400 (100%) thru 380 (95%)—PASS.** Perfect. He is an Adult, and a Man. He has mastered all the Adult skills. He is ready to learn to teach other males to be Adults. Ladies, this is the Man you will want to marry if he passes all his other Manhood tests.

- **379 (94%) thru 360 (90%)—PASS.** He is an Adult, but needs some polish on a few of the Adult skills to score higher if you want a perfect Man. Ladies, this Man is nearly perfect. So, you may be the type of Woman who likes a dash of bad boy mixed in her perfect Man type. And you will fall in love with him.

- **359 (89%) thru 320 (80%)—FAIL.** More boy than Man. Remedial training required on many Adult skills.

- **319 (79%) thru 280 (70%)—FAIL.** He's a little baby. He could try to master the Adult skills, but maybe does not want to put out the effort. He is probably very happy and comfortable living the spoiled brat lifestyle, preferring that his mommy takes care of him.

- **279 (69%) thru 240 (60%)—FAIL.** Definitely a boy who may never make Manhood. Chronically infected with P-Syndrome. May not be curable. Most likely got zero points in several adult skills, low points in others, and needs immediate remedial training in most of the skills.

- **239 (59%) thru 0 (0%)—FAIL.** 100% candy-ass, little baby. This guy has terminal PS that will eventually kill him. He is a first class loser who has chosen to be a baby. He does not intend to master any of the adult skills, thus has no chance to achieve adulthood and be a Man. His best career move is to become an organ donor. Somebody eventually will put a bullet in his head or shank him in prison.

APPENDIX 4: SKILLS CHECKLIST — CITIZEN, 3RD ED.

1. Loyal Citizen
2. Involved Citizen
3. Obeys the Law
4. Respects Authority
5. Speaks English
6. Understands Basic Government
7. Respects Community
8. Stands Up for Rights
9. Cross Culturalism
10. Votes
11. Community Service
12. Knows Who Is Running the Government
13. Constitution
14. Knows What's Going on in the World
15. Good Neighbor
16. Code of Conduct
17. Member of Professional Organization
18. Support the Military
19. Noble Cause

APPENDIX 5: MANHOOD TEST #2 — CITIZEN, 3RD ED.

Once all the training is completed, the next step is Manhood Test #2 — Citizen.

NOTE: Once the infrastructure is in place the man being tested must have passed the adult test beforehand, and possess a valid man card. No exceptions.

The test is administered by a minimum of three adults, who have intimate knowledge of the male's training and preparation for citizenship. Test administrators should include a combination of parents, teachers, clergy, or elders. The Man being assessed should be present in case a test administrator wishes to ask the boy any questions.

Administer this test periodically before the boy turns 18 to determine where his weak areas are for further training. The official test is taken between 17 ½ and 19 ½ years old. If he fails the Citizen test, he must participate in remedial training. Once he has been deemed ready to take the test again, the entire examination will be administered once more.

DIRECTIONS TO TEST ADMINISTRATOR:
1. Read all 19 questions.
2. Score each question 0 to 10 points.
3. Total the score (190 points maximum).
4. Use the scoring chart at the end of the test to determine the final results and the status of the tested male.

SCORING TIPS: You can score each question from zero (0) to a maximum of ten (10) points. When evaluating the question, consider whether or not the male you are testing has 100% succeeded on a particular question; that's 10 points. If he is near perfect then that is an 8 or 9. If the guy is missing a important part of the skill, that is 3 to 7 points. If he is nearly failing, that is 1 or 2 points. And finally, if this guy you're testing is clueless on a skill, or just totally failing, that is ZERO points. Your objectivity comes into play. The bottom line is your scoring will determine if this guy is an Adult and a Citizen ... or not. Be hard, be ruthless in your scoring. We cannot allow any male who is not ready to slip through.

Mastering Citizen skills and passing the second Manhood Test is a rite-of-passage. If you pass a Man, and he fails to perform as a Citizen, you may have to explain why you passed him. The test must take years to prepare for and be difficult, but not impossible, to pass. Remember, no matter how hard we train and mentor, preparing our boys for the test, some guys were just never meant to be Citizens. A certain percentage will be chronic failures for a variety of reasons.

19 multipart questions. 10 points each. 190 points total.

1. LOYAL CITIZEN. Is the Man a loyal citizen? Is he faithful to his country, his promises and commitments, and anyone he gives his word to? Is he a traitor?
2. INVOLVED CITIZEN. Is the Man an involved citizen? Does

he step up to help his community and his country?

3. OBEY THE LAW. Does the Man obey the law? Does he have a "spirit-of-the-law" philosophy?

4. RESPECTS AUTHORITY. Does the Man respect authority?

5. SPEAKS ENGLISH. Does the Man speak, read, and write English fluently enough to fulfill his duties as a Man?

6. UNDERSTANDS BASIC GOVERNMENT. Does the Man understand the basic structure of Federal, State, and local Government and how they work? If applicable, has he taken and passed the Citizenship Test?

7. RESPECTS COMMUNITY. Does the Man treat his community, and its members, with respect and courtesy? Does he keep his community clean? Does he litter?

8. STANDS UP FOR RIGHTS. Does the Man stand up for his rights and the rights of others?

9. CROSS CULTURALISM. Does the Man understand, respect, and enjoy the cultural and ethnic similarities and differences among those who live here?

10. VOTES. Is the Man registered to vote no matter where he is in the world? Does he vote in all elections? Is he a member of a political party?

11. COMMUNITY SERVICE. Does the Man participate in some form of community service in his local neighborhood, his state, or his country?

12. KNOWS WHO IS RUNNING THE GOVERNMENT. Does the Man know who all the government key players are: local, state, and federal representatives/public officials?

13. CONSTITUTION. Has the Man read the U.S. Constitution, Bill of Rights, and Declaration of Independence? Does he understand the significance of those documents?

14. KNOWS WHAT'S GOING ON IN THE WORLD. Does he know what is going on in the world? Does he read the news, and keep informed of world, regional, and local news events? Does he pay attention to government and geopolitics?

15. GOOD NEIGHBOR. Is the Man a good neighbor? Does he personally know his neighbors? Is he helpful to his neighbors and protective of his neighborhood?

16. CODE OF CONDUCT. Does the Man live by a code of conduct? Does he have a set of rules outlining responsibilities and good behavior for a Man?

17. MEMBER OF PROFESSIONAL ORGANIZATION. Is the Man a member of a professional organization?
18. SUPPORT THE MILITARY. Does the Man support the military?
19. NOBLE CAUSE. Does the Man engage in a noble cause?

SCORING, MANHOOD TEST #2 — CITIZEN, 3rd Ed.

- **190 (100%) thru 180 (95%)—PASS.** Perfect. He is a loyal and involved citizen. He has mastered all the Citizen skills.

- **179 (94%) thru 171 (90%)—PASS.** He is a Citizen with just a touch of rebelliousness. Needs only some polish on a few of the citizen skills to make him perfect.

- **170 (89%) thru 152 (80%)—FAIL.** Probably did not pass the Adult test either. Remedial training required on many citizen skills.

- **151 (79%) thru 133 (70%)—FAIL.** He's a welfare recipient. He could try to master the citizen skills, but he probably has not passed the Adult test. He is probably very happy and comfortable living off the taxpayers.

- **132 (69%) thru 114 (60%)—FAIL.** Definitely on government assistance. A boy who may never make manhood. Chronically infected with PS. May not be curable. Most likely flunked the Adult test more than once.

- **113 (59%) thru 0 (0%)—FAIL.** This guy is a homeless drug addict ... by choice since his parents had to throw him out of the house because of his chronic unemployment and drug addiction.

APPENDIX 6: MANHOOD SKILLS CHECKLIST
— PRE-HUSBAND, 1ST ED.

1.   *Have a job.*
2.   *True love*
3.   *Committed Relationship*
4.   *Fatherhood & Children*
5.   *Neat & Clean*
6.   *Personality*
7.   *Money*
8.   *Sex*
9.   *Education & Intelligence*
10. *Friendship*
11. *Communication*
12. *Low Maintenance*
13. *Common Interests*
14. *Family & Friends*
15. *Good Character*
16. *Mommy & "ex's"*
17. *Passed Adult & Citizen Manhood Tests*
18. *Well Mannered*
19. *Control Freak*
20. *Spirituality*

APPENDIX 7: MANHOOD BONUS TEST —
PRE-HUSBAND, 3ᴿᴰ ED.

This supplemental test is very different from all of the other Manhood tests. The test is administered by a single woman to validate if the Man she is testing could be a loving and faithful Husband to her. It will help her decide how to answer he should propose marriage.

NOTE: Once the infrastructure is in place the man being tested must have passed the adult and citizen tests beforehand, and possess a valid man card. No exceptions.

DIRECTIONS TO TEST ADMINISTRATOR:
1. Test is administered by a woman verifying if the Man she is testing will make a loving and faithful Husband.

2. This test may be administered with or without the Man being examined present.
3. Other women who have enough knowledge of the Man may administer this test. The more women who administer the test, the more the test's accuracy will increase.
4. Read to yourself all 20 questions.
5. Score each question 0 to 10 points.
6. Total the score (200 points maximum).
7. Use the scoring chart at the end of the test to determine the final results and the status of the tested male.

SCORING TIPS: You can score each question from zero (0) to a maximum of ten (10) points. When evaluating the question, consider whether the male you are testing has 100% succeeded on a particular question; that's 10 points. If he is nearly perfect, then that is an 8 or 9. If the guy is missing an important part of the skill, that is 3 to 7 points. If he is nearly failing, that is 1 or 2 points. And finally, if this guy you're testing is clueless on a skill, or just totally failing, that is ZERO points. Your objectivity comes into play.

The bottom line is your scoring will determine if this guy is husband material worth falling in love with ... or not. Be hard, be ruthless in your scoring. We cannot allow any male who is not ready to slip through.

Test him weekly, if necessary, to determine if he is scoring higher.

20 questions. 10 points each. 200 points total.
1. HAVE A JOB. Does he have a job? Does he have a clear career/life plan that maps out his goals as to where he is going in his life? Is marriage in his plan?
2. TRUE LOVE. Does he truly love you? Does he make you feel appreciated and respected for all you do for him? Does he make you happy?
3. COMMITTED RELATIONSHIP. Does he desire a committed relationship? Do you feel that you have picked your prince, the man with whom you wish to live for the rest of your life?
4. FATHERHOOD and CHILDREN. Does he want children? Is he, or does he want to be, a father? Does he possess the skills

and aptitude necessary to be a patient and caring Father?

5. NEAT and CLEAN. Is he neat and clean: body, clothing, car, home, work, etc? Is he well groomed, organized, reliable, and punctual?

6. PERSONALITY. His overall personality: usually upbeat, humorous, rarely moody? He handles stress well and is a calming force in the relationship?

7. MONEY. He earns enough money to live decently? Does he manage his money and credit well? Does he have a financial plan?

8. SEX. Does he make it fun, satisfying, and stress-free? Does he manage his horniness very well? Does he have eyes only for you?

9. EDUCATION and INTELLIGENCE. Is he intelligent and educated enough? Or is he a stupid ignorant fool? Does he consider you to be intelligent, even smarter than he is? Or does he think you are stupid?

10. FRIENDSHIP. Can he be emotionally available to you? Are you his most trusted, best friend? Does he like people and does he like the company of others?

11. COMMUNICATION. Does he communicate well with you? Is he genuinely easy to talk to? Is he an effective listener? Does he take and give criticism well?

12. LOW MAINTENANCE. Is he low maintenance? Is it easy for you to keep him happy? Does he enjoy life? Any mental disorders, issues or addictions?

13. COMMON INTERESTS. Do you and he share common interests? Does he share his interests with you so you can enjoy them if you choose to?

14. FAMILY and FRIENDS. Do his family and friends like and accept you? Do your family and friends like and accept him? His mom likes you? Your dad likes him?

15. GOOD CHARACTER. Is he a man of good character? Is he trustworthy, respectful, fair, caring, self-confident, and kind?

16. MOMMY and "EXs." Does he have any "mommy" or ex-girlfriend/wife issues? Any baby-mama, or children issues that interfere with the relationship?

17. PASSED ADULT and CITIZEN MANHOOD TESTS. Has he passed Manhood Tests #1 and #2 — Adult and Citizen? Does he possess a valid Man Card? **NOTE:** Until the infrastructure

is in place to administer the Adult and Citizen Manhood Tests, give him ten points on the test.

18. WELL MANNERED. Is he well mannered and polite? Or does he constantly embarrass you with his stupid immature behavior?

19. CONTROL FREAK. Is he an egotistical, narcissistic, control freak? Can he be a good family leader?

20. SPIRITUALITY. Is religion/spirituality important in your life? Are you and he close to the same viewpoint on religion and spirituality?

SCORING, BONUS MANHOOD TEST — PRE-HUSBAND, 3rd Ed.

- **200 (100%) thru 190 (95%)—PASS.** He is a man! He is perfect! Marry him now! Say "I do" before your girlfriend with this checklist hooks him.

- **189 (94%) thru 180 (90%)—PASS.** Marry later! Needs only some polish. Ladies considering him for husband material should take more time with this guy before telling him she loves him. When he shines up to 95%, marry him.

- **170 (89%) thru 160 (80%)—FAIL.** Don't marry him! You could test him longer to see if he can score higher. But, he most likely will disappoint you. If he can't pick up enough points fairly quickly, don't screw around, dump him!

- **159 (79%) thru 140 (70%)—FAIL.** Dump him! Males who score in this range tend to be ignorant, whiny, couch potatoes, unemployed, living with parents, and lazy. Ladies, don't let him move in and don't loan him money. He's a loser who will take advantage of you.

- **139 (69%) thru 120 (60%)—FAIL.** Dump him immediately! He is an SOB and way too creepy. A psycho-stalker, mental defective, and a parasite who will steal your money, your car, and your heart.

- **119 (59%) thru 0 (0%)—FAIL.** Run away! He is a total

bastard, ex-con, drug addict, dirt bag, etc. He is scary. Get a restraining order and buy a gun. Consider getting into the witness protection program.

APPENDIX 8: MANHOOD SKILLS CHECKLIST -- HUSBAND, 1ST ED.

1.   *Love*
2.   *Faithfulness*
3.   *Understands Marriage*
4.   *Marriage Is Teamwork*
5.   *Can Handle Money*
6.   *Provider*
7.   *Wife Is His Best Friend*
8.   *Pamper Your Wife*
9.   *Husband Character Traits*
10. *Leadership*
11. *Sex & Affection*
12. *Jealousy*
13. *Communication*
14. *Control*
15. *Protector*
16. *Values*

APPENDIX 9: MANHOOD TEST #3 — HUSBAND, 3RD ED.

Once all the training is completed, the next step is to administer Manhood Test #3 — Husband. Since this is the third Manhood test, one would expect that, having passed three previous tests of Manhood, the Man being tested is fully prepared and ready to pass the Husband test.

The test is administered by the fiancé or wife, and at least two other adults who have intimate knowledge of the Man's training and preparation for becoming a Husband. The Man being assessed should be present in case a test administrator wishes to ask him any questions. A Man can be tested repeatedly until he can pass the examination.

Administer this test periodically starting when the Man is officially engaged to determine where his weak areas are for further training. The official test is administered before the wedding.

After the wedding, the Man should be tested at a minimum of every 2 years just to make sure he is fulfilling his duties as a loving and faithful Husband.

NOTE: Once the infrastructure is in place the man being tested must have passed the adult, citizen, and pre-husband tests beforehand, and possess a valid man card. No exceptions.

DIRECTIONS TO TEST ADMINISTRATOR:
1. Read all 16 questions.
2. Score each question 0 to 10 points.
3. Total the score (160 points maximum).
4. Use the scoring chart at the end of the test to determine the final results and the status of the tested male.

SCORING TIPS: You can score each question from zero (0) to a maximum of ten (10) points. When evaluating the question, consider whether the Man you are testing has 100% succeeded on a particular question; that's 10 points. If he is near perfect then that is an 8 or 9. If the Man is missing a important part of the skill, that is 3 to 7 points. If he is nearly failing, that is 1 or 2 points. And finally, if this Man you are testing is clueless on a skill, or just totally failing, that is ZERO points. Your objectivity comes into play. The bottom line is your scoring will determine if this Man is Husband material ... or not. Be hard, be ruthless in your scoring. We cannot allow any Man who is not ready to slip through.

16 multipart questions. 10 points each. 160 points total.

1. LOVE. Is the Man a loving Husband? Does he make his Wife feel genuinely loved and cared for? Does he regularly tell his Wife he loves her, and that she is beautiful? Does the Husband tell his Wife that he is the luckiest Man in the world that she is his Wife? Does the Man honor his Wife in public by making her feel like she is the only woman in his world and the center

of his universe? Does the Wife "like" her Husband?

2. FAITHFULNESS. Is the Husband faithful to his wife? Is he an adulterer? Does the Husband tell his Wife how lucky he is that she said yes when he proposed? Is the Husband flirtatious with other females, disrespecting his Wife? Is the Husband in full control of his libido?

3. UNDERSTANDS MARRIAGE. Does the husband put his marriage vows first? Does he respect his marriage? Does the Husband understand and accept that a marriage evolves and changes over time, passing through different stages? Does the Husband treat his marriage as the most important part of his life, over career, friends, and his family?

4. MARRIAGE IS TEAMWORK. Does the Husband make his marriage a real partnership with his Wife? Or does he treat her as a second class citizen? Or a slave?

5. CAN HANDLE MONEY. Does the Husband handle money well? Does he ensure his Wife is cared for and not deprived? Does he keep his family financially sound? Is there always enough money for the household to live comfortably on? Does the Husband strike a balance in spending, never frivolously spending their money, yet never being a tightwad? Does the Husband team with his Wife to jointly manage the family finances? Does the Husband insist that the Wife and the Husband make the big money decisions together? If the Wife is the primary money manager, does the Husband trust in her money management skills?

6. PROVIDER. Is the Husband able to properly provide for his family? Is he self-motivated, ambitious, and does he have a clear plan on how to best provide for his family? Does he earn enough money that his Wife does not have to work unless she wants to? When this is applicable, if she does work, does the Husband insist she use the money she earns as she wants, not just to pay household bills? In today's two income households, do both the Wife and the Husband respectfully possess an equal say and an equal vote in the disbursement of the jointly earned funds? Is the agreement of who the provider is and who the stay at home parent is a mutually acceptable agreement? Is the Husband a hard working Man?

7. WIFE IS HIS BEST FRIEND. Is the Husband his Wife's very best friend? Does the Husband take full advantage of, have

full appreciation of, and constantly learn from his wife's communication and empathy skills? Can the Husband tell his wife anything? Does the Husband trust his Wife to keep his secrets he shares with her? Does he enjoy talking to her about the "happenings of the day?" Does the Husband care about how his Wife is feeling? Does the Husband give his Wife space for the other relationships in her life, such as her parents, family, friends, and colleagues?

8. PAMPER YOUR WIFE. Does the Husband pamper his loving, hard working Wife? Does he regularly tell his wife that she is beautiful, especially when she has changed her look, or is wearing her hair differently, or has a new outfit? Does he make her feel guilty for spending money on makeup and nice clothes to look pretty for her Man? Does the Husband encourage his Wife to grow as an individual? Does he give her thoughtful gifts on all of the important days: wedding anniversary, her birthday, Valentine's Day, Christmas, and any other day designated as special? Does he give her little surprise gifts at other times? Does the Husband make special times for his wife to share experiences, thoughts, and feelings in a positive manner? Is he there for her when she feels down?

9. HUSBAND CHARACTER TRAITS. Does the Husband have confidence and a sense of self-worth? Does the Husband have positive self-esteem and self-image? Is he narcissistic, arrogant, or overly confident to the point of being reckless or negligent? Is the Husband self-disciplined and goal oriented? Does he use his maturity and self-discipline to avoid temptation, such as adultery, drug addictions, etc? Does he use his self-control to keep from losing his temper? Does the Husband respect his Wife's intelligence and capabilities? Does he know his wife wants to feel appreciated and respected by him? Is the Husband quick to apologize? Is he magnanimous, forgiving his Wife for her failings as well as atoning for his shortcomings and mistakes? Is the Husband kind and gentle with his Wife? Is the Husband loyal to his Wife? Is the Husband reliable?

10. LEADERSHIP. Is the Husband an effective family leader? Or is he a controlling jerk? Can the husband adapt to life's changes? Is he sensitive to how those changes affect his family and can he roll with it? Is the Husband fair?

11. SEX and AFFECTION. Does the Husband keep his wife happy

in bed? Does he make sex fun and stress free? Does he enjoy himself with her? Does he make sure that they communicate about their love making so that they can maximize each other's pleasure? Is the Husband affectionate? Does he know that his Wife enjoys the non-sexual, physical contact of her Husband? Does he give her hugs and kisses? Does he hold her hand or take her arm when walking in public? Does he like to snuggle? Does the husband know what his wife enjoys in the bedroom?

12. JEALOUSY. Does the Husband get jealous? Is he faithful to his wife and trusts her to be faithful to him? Did the husband bring any emotional baggage into the marriage? Does he ever compare his wife to his mother, ex-girlfriends, ex-wives, or baby-mamas?

13. COMMUNICATION. Has the Husband mastered the Adult skill of interpersonal communication? Does he always share hassle-free communication with his Wife? Is he always open and honest with his Wife, keeping her informed on everything? Does he make time to talk with her daily? Does he prevent distractions from inhibiting their communication? Has he mastered the adult skill of effective listening and has he refined that skill for effectively communicating with his Wife? Does the Husband accept that his Wife may only want her Husband to listen to her and not try to fix her problem? Or does he jump right in disrespectfully and mettle? Does the Husband accept that his Wife, as a woman, sometimes needs to verbalize her life? Does he just listen or try to "manage" her?

14. CONTROL. Does the Husband have an obsessive need to be in control of everything that is happening? Does he enjoy and appreciate living with a Wife who has strong opinions? A wife who a sense of self-worth, and has her own individual life, friends, career, hobbies, and pursuits?

15. PROTECTOR. Does the Husband make his Wife feel safe and secure? Does she feel he will protect her from harm?

16. VALUES. Does the Husband team with his Wife to establish and maintain sound values for their marriage and family?

SCORING, MANHOOD TEST #3 — HUSBAND, 3rd Ed.

- **160 (100%) thru 152 (95%)—PASS.** He is the perfect Husband. The Wife should keep him and do all she can to keep him happy. If the Man is not yet engaged, then the woman who desires him had better get a ring on her finger fast before some other women hooks this Man.

- **151 (94%) thru 144 (90%)—PASS.** This Man is almost the perfect Husband, but, with a few rough spots, that should make him a "normal" dad.

- **143 (89%) thru 128 (80%)—FAIL.** This Male has enough issues that they distract him from being a good Husband. He may, or may not be salvageable. If he has passed the Adult, Citizen, and Pre-Husband tests, he may just need more training to pass this test. If he has flunked one or more of the first three tests, he is not Husband material yet. A woman should say "no" if he proposes.

- **127 (79%) thru 112 (70%)—FAIL.** Don't marry this Man. Dump him! Males who score in this range probably never took, or flunked, the Adult, Citizen and Pre-Husband tests. This Man needs to remain single and train hard to pass the test.

- **111 (69%) thru 96 (60%)—FAIL.** Dump him immediately! He should never have been allowed to take this test. He probably never passed the first three manhood tests.

- **95 (59%) thru 0 (0%)—FAIL.** Total bastard. Not a Man. Not a Citizen. Don't even think about falling in love with this SOB.

APPENDIX 10: MANHOOD SKILLS CHECKLIST -- FATHER, 1ST ED.

1. *Patience*
2. *Caring*
3. *Fun Dad*
4. *Disciplinarian*
5. *Time*
6. *Leadership*
7. *Teacher/Trainer*
8. *Parenting*
9. *Love*
10. *Protector*
11. *Father Character Traits*
12. *Communication*
13. *Responsibility*
14. *Reasonable Expectations*
15. *Not Mean*
16. *Wise With Money*
17. *Values*

APPENDIX 11: MANHOOD TEST # 4 — FATHER, 4th. Ed.

Once all the training is completed, the next step is to administer Manhood Test #4 — Father. Since this is the fourth Manhood test, one would expect that, having passed three previous tests of Manhood, the Man being tested is fully prepared and ready to pass the Father test.

The test is administered by the Wife and at least two other adults who have intimate knowledge of the Man's training and preparation for becoming a Father. The Man being assessed should be present in case a test administrator wishes to ask him any questions. A Man can be tested repeatedly until he can pass the examination.

This test should be first administered when the Husband and Wife are working on their plan for when, and how many, children to have. His official test is administered when his Wife has announced the pregnancy. After the birth, the Man should be tested at a minimum of every 2 years just to make sure he is fulfilling his duties as a patient and caring Father.

NOTE: Once the infrastructure is in place the man being tested must have passed the adult, citizen, pre-husband, and Husband tests beforehand, and possess a valid man card. No exceptions.

DIRECTIONS TO TEST ADMINISTRATOR:
1. Read all 17 questions.
2. Score each question 0 to 10 points.
3. Total the score (170 points maximum).
4. Use the scoring chart at the end of the test to determine the final results and the status of the tested male.

SCORING TIPS: You can score each question from zero (0) to a maximum of ten (10) points. When evaluating the question, consider whether the Man you are testing has 100% succeeded on a particular question; that's 10 points. If he is near perfect then that is an 8 or 9. If the Man is missing an important part of the skill, that is 3 to 7 points. If he is nearly failing, that is 1 or 2 points. And finally, if this Man you are testing is clueless on a skill, or just totally failing, that is ZERO points. Your objectivity comes into play. The bottom line is your scoring will determine if this Man is Father material ... or not. Be hard, be ruthless in your scoring. We cannot allow any Man who is not ready to slip through.

17 multipart questions. 10 points each. 170 points total.

1. PATIENCE. Has the Father mastered the skill of patience, to accept or tolerate delay, trouble, or suffering without getting angry or upset? Can he keep his temper under control? Can the father appear calm under fire, in full control of his emotions? Is he the calming force for his family?
2. CARING. Is the Father kind and does he show genuine interest in others? Is he friendly and approachable? Is he is generous with his time for his children?
3. FUN DAD. Is he—or will he be when his kids are born—a fun dad? Does he have a sense of humor? Or does he take life too seriously all the time? Does he like to sometimes just

run around and have fun? Can he be called a "fun dad?" Does he love to play with his kids? Is the Father a funny guy who makes his kids laugh all the time? Does the Father believe his kids are the coolest people to have fun with? Does the Father initiate fun family trips? Does he establish family traditions, such as opening one present on Christmas Eve?

4. DISCIPLINARIAN. Is the Father a fair and effective disciplinarian? Is he the chief family disciplinarian? Does he work together with the Mother on the family discipline program so that punishments are issued fairly and consistently for each child? Does the Father accept that each child is a unique individual with a distinct personality, thus requiring that punishment for the same family crime may be different for each child? Has the Father mastered all the punishment tools in his disciplinary toolbox, such as time-outs, isolation, verbal reprimands, and corporal punishment? Is the Father the final disciplinary authority for his sons?

5. TIME. Does the Father devote lots of time to be with his children? Does he know that he is building an emotional bond with his children, absolutely comprehending each child's unique individual personality? Does the Father know how to have fun and has he not lost his ability to act like a kid? Does the Father take the time to listen and to talk with his kids? Is he approachable and easy to talk with?

6. LEADERSHIP. Does the Father accept that the skill of leadership is much more complex as the Father than as a Husband? That it can be unquestionably more challenging as a Father? Is the Father a good family leader? Is the Father the role model to his family, displaying his good and bad habits? Does the Father teach leadership, followership, mission focus, and teamwork to his children, especially to his sons so they can pass the Manhood Adult and Citizen Tests? Does the Father stick around or run away like a coward? Does the Father trust his children?

7. TEACHER/TRAINER. Does the Father train his sons to be mature and responsible Adults? Does he prepare his sons to pass the Adult Manhood Test at 18 years old? Does he assist his Wife in training his daughters to be mature and responsible Adults? Does the Father challenge his children to do their very best at home, in school, and in their lives? Does the Father

expect his children to make mistakes and does he encourage self-improvement within them? Does he teach his children to be self-motivated and to have a healthy self-esteem, confidence in their own merit as an individual person?

8. PARENTING. Has the Father mastered the skill of parenting, the process of preparing his children to be mature and responsible Adults, and loyal and involved Citizens? Is he responsible for his sons completing their rite-of-passage—from "boy" to "Man"—by preparing them to pass the Adult Manhood Test? Does the Father hold on to the parenting mistakes committed by his parents? Does the Father fully comprehend the dangers of favoritism, the preferring of one child over one or more of his other children? Does the Father avoid showing favoritism by spreading out his love, good humor, and leadership equally to the entire family? Can the Father admit his flaws so that his kids will learn by example?

9. LOVE. Does the Father make the family feel deeply loved? Will he do anything for his family? Does he love his children when they succeed, and when they fail? Does the Father show his affection in front of his family, showering them with hugs and kisses and "I love you?" Does he encourage his family to do well, to be happy, and to find joy in life? Does the Father share his love so openly that his whole family feels loved and appreciated? Does the Father ensure his children know he loves them and will be there for them no matter what happens?

10. PROTECTOR. Is the Father the family protector? Has he mastered the skill of family security? Does he take responsibility for the safety and security of the home and all members of his family, whether they are at home or away from it? Does the Father act unreasonably overly protective?

11. FATHER CHARACTER TRAITS. Does the Father love to stimulate his children to new things, new ideas, and new places? Does he get excited when sharing with his kids the big, wide, wonderful world out there? Does he train his children to appreciate their mother, their home, their school, their community, etc? Does he ever let his children take what they have for granted? Is the Father open-minded, free from negatives bias, receptive to new ideas and to change? Does he allow his kids to be members of the society and the culture of their day and age? Is he supportive and passionately loyal

to his family? Is the Father his children's public defender, standing by them when needed?

12. COMMUNICATION. Has the Father mastered the adult skill of interpersonal communication? Does the Father comprehend that there is a special communication between Father and child? Is the Father an outstanding communicator with his children? Does he listen to them? Does the Father ensure his children feel that Dad is always interested in them?

13. RESPONSIBILITY. Does the Father accept full responsibility for the well-being and proper rearing of his children?

14. REASONABLE EXPECTATIONS. Does the Father have reasonable expectations for his children based on who they are as individuals? Does the Father try to achieve his childhood goals which he could not accomplish during his own childhood through his kids?

15. NOT MEAN. Is the Father mean or cruel to his family? Is he is a nice guy most of the time? Is he ever abusive or neglectful?

16. WISE WITH MONEY. Is the Father wise with money? Does he earn enough money to take care of his family? Does he manage and budget his money, working together on this with his Wife? Is the Father a good, "family money" manager? Does he teach his children, early on, the adult skill of money management to prepare them to earn and manage their own money?

17. VALUES. Does the Father establish sound family values to guide his children? Does the Father teach his children right from wrong? And how to develop one's own individual moral compass? Doe he value setting family standards, the family mission, and its goals? Does he value the rewards of hard work and the developing of a work ethic?

SCORING, MANHOOD TEST #4 — FATHER, 4th Ed.

- **170 (100%) thru 161 (95%)—PASS.** This Man is "Father of the year." He is the perfect Father. The Wife will love being married to this man and making beautiful children with him. Ladies, if you are not married to this man, then you had better do it quickly.

- **160 (94%) thru 153 (90%)—PASS**. This man is more like "Father of the month" six months of the year. He is almost perfect but will growl at the kids sometimes, making him a "normal" Dad. If you have not married this man, again, do it quickly.

- **142 (89%) thru 136 (80%)—FAIL.** Maybe "Father of the month" once every couple of years. This male has enough issues that they distract him from being a good father. He has got about a 50%-50% chance of getting his act together to pass the Father Manhood Test. Don't even think about getting pregnant with him until he passes the test.

- **135 (79%) thru 119 (70%)—FAIL.** Don't make any babies with him. Dump him! Males who score in this range tend to be ignorant, unemployed, and lazy. He is a loser who will take advantage of you.

- **118 (69%) thru 102 (60%)—FAIL.** NO Babies. Dump him immediately!

- **101 (59%) thru 0 (0%)—FAIL.** Run away! He is a total bastard. As with the other tests, get a restraining order and buy a gun. If you made children with this loser, then consider getting the family into the witness protection program.

APPENDIX 12: RITE-OF-PASSAGE CEREMONY --GENERAL PLANNING

PRE-GAME
- Test Completed—Man being tested is present for questioning by the test administrators. There are usually three test proctors.
- Oral Interview—Man interviewed by test administrators.
- At the end of the oral interview the Man is authorized to get his Man tattoo. Added tattooing for each test passed.

GAME DAY
- Invocation
- Flag ceremony
- Host comments
- Man or Men introduced to audience

- Men show their tattoos
- Each Man makes a short speech thanking those Men who trained him and did not kill him instead.
- Men are awarded their Man Cards and Manhood Credential. For later rituals, their cards are endorsed for Husband and Father.
- Hugs and back slaps all around
- The Man Toast
- Benediction
- More cheering, applause, back slapping
- Buffet Line and Bar open after benediction
- The smoking lamp is lit.

POST-GAME
- Man Card briefing
- Duties briefing
- Next step briefing
- Report

APPENDIX 13: RITE-OF-PASSAGE CEREMONY #1—ADULT, 2ND ED.

PRE-GAME
- Biggest ritual of the four ceremonies.
- May need large room or hall.
- Location must accommodate buffet and bar.
- Plan on more than one boy participant. Up to 10 boys is a good number.
- Each new Man must read his career/life plan on Game Day. Make sure the boy did a good job. If a plan is thought to be weak, Men are allowed to throw things at the new Man reading his plan.
- Adult tattoo is the largest and most painful section of the four part Man tattoo. There are three more tattoo elements that make up the complete Man tattoo.
- Get tattoo done and healed so it can be displayed on Game Day.

GAME DAY
- Should have guest speaker.
- This will be a drinking event. No attendees drive. Transport is prearranged by the host. All attendees drinking must have a Wing-man.
- Gifts are given: usually money, alcohol, guns, or cars.
- After the Man Toast, the Man removes his scrotum, lays it on the table, hits it with a hammer, hands the hammer to the host, who hits the Man's sack as hard as he can. Then the Man's Father whacks the sack, maybe a couple more invited Men whack the sack. The Man is not allowed to cry, yell, or scream. He must show great courage, concentration, and will power by remaining completely silent, still, and calm. When the hammering is completed, the Man picks up his sack, straps it back on, where it stays for the rest of his life.
- Use the special ceremonial hammer or mallet only.

I'm joking about the sack whacking. If you actually read that I was joking, then contact me with code word "Nuts." The tattoo is my pain component. Not everyone will read this far.

POST-GAME
- Lots of ice for the graduates.

APPENDIX 14: RITE-OF-PASSAGE CEREMONY #2—CITIZEN, 2ND ED.

PRE-GAME
- Registers to vote. Bring proof on Game Day.
- Game usually held with Adult rite.
- Proof of at least 800 hours of community service is required.
- The Man gets the "Citizen" section of the Man tattoo.

GAME DAY
- American flag is on-site.
- New Citizen will lead the pledge of allegiance.
- New Citizen will sing the Star Spangled Banner a capella.

POST-GAME
- Votes at every election.

APPENDIX 15: RITE-OF-PASSAGE, CEREMONY #3—HUSBAND/WEDDING, 2ND ED.

PRE-GAME
- Ceremony held at the Wedding location.
- Make sure the ritual is on the wedding schedule.
- Plan for 3 to 5 hours for the event.
- Arrange for food and beverages at the ritual location on Game Day.
- The Man gets the "Husband" section of the Man tattoo.

GAME DAY
- Rite is held while the bride is preparing on her wedding day.
- Bridal preparation time is 6 to 12 hours.
- The rite is hosted by the Best Man.
- Attended by all the groomsmen as well as all the Men attending the wedding: Fathers, uncles, brothers, cousins and male friends of the Bride and Groom.
- After the Man Toast, the Man being advanced to Husband, holds out his scrotum, his Best Man kneels down in front of the Groom and gently kisses the Groom's sack for failing at the tradition of talking the Groom out of getting married before his wedding day. After the kissing, the Man puts his sack away and heads for the altar.
- Event is done when Groom, Best Man, and groomsmen are called to the altar. All other Men who attended the ceremony return to their seats.

I was joking about the sack kissing. If you actually read that I was joking, then contact me with code word "Nuts." There is no need for the Best Man to try to talk the Groom out of getting married, because the Groom is a Man. And a Man always picks the perfect women to be his Wife.

POST-GAME
- Post Honeymoon celebration of new couple.
- With beer & honeymoon photos
- Carry-bride-over-threshold ceremony

APPENDIX 16: RITE-OF-PASSAGE CEREMONY #4—FATHER , 2ND ED.

PRE-GAME
- This event can be held in a bar, someone's house, or at the hospital where the newborn baby is located.
- When the wife is pregnant, Game planning starts.
- Get good cigars.
- Appetizers, fast food, or sliders are the best food choice for this ritual.
- Man gets Father part of the Man tattoo.

GAME DAY
- The actual game day is the day the Father's first child is born.
- The ritual can be held as soon as possible after the delivery date.
- No "sack" ritual as the Man will watch live, his Wife go through childbirth.
- Baby viewing.
- Father is awarded a whacking stick.
- Buffet and bar open
- Smoking lamp is lit for special cigars.

POST-GAME
- Send photos of new baby to all Men. Include all the birth info.
- Also send funniest "in labor" photo of Wife.

APPENDIX 17: MAN CARD --
PROTOTYPE MOCK-UP

Every Man who passes the Adult test is awarded his Man Card at the first Rite-of-Passage ceremony. With this card he is entitled to certain privileges available only to Men. Such as drinking beer, eating meat, watching TV, cursing, & access to women. Women can't talk to a male over age of 18 who does not have a valid Man Card. She would not want to talk to an idiot without his Man Card anyway. The Man Card can be revoked for failure to pass tests or failure to perform the duties of a Man.

MAN CARD

WF-028764209940   EXPIRES 09-27-2016

Dudley Manley
909 Amce Drive
Sacramento, CA 95345

HT: 5-09   WT: 595   HAIR: Brn   EYES: Grn

RESTRICTIONS: None

Dudley D. Manly, 02-28-2012

By his signature, the Man listed on the front of this card swears has passed the Manhood Test(s) listed below. He acknowledges that, under penalty of having this privileges revoked and this card confiscated, that he will faithfully carry out the duties of a Man for which he has been tested.

MANHOOD TEST, DATE PASSED/DATE REVOKED

- Adult   _____   _____
- Citizen   _____   _____
- Husband   _____   _____
- Father   _____   _____

The bearer of this card is a Man. Unless sooner revoked, he is entitled to enjoy the privileges of Manhood. To included, but not limited to: access to women, use of intoxicating substances, able to use profanity when appropriate, watch television and movies, use computers the internet purely for entertainment, eat meat, etc.

APPENDIX 18: CHARACTER TRAITS—ADULT

1. Caring
2. Charming
3. Chivalrous
4. Common Sense
5. Courage
6. Courtesy
7. Follower
8. Generosity
9. Good Decision-making
10. Good self esteem
11. Humility
12. Integrity/Trustworthiness
13. Kindness
14. Leadership
15. Loyalty
16. Motivated
17. Obedience
18. Patience
19. Respect for others & self respect
20. Responsibility
21. Self-Confidence
22. Self-Discipline
23. Sincerity
24. Sound Judgment
25. Team work
26. Work ethic

This list is more comprehensive than in chapter 3. I tried to capture every character trait I could think of for an adult. If you think I am missing some. Or you don't think one should be on this list, email me. Gallantry@lanset.com

APPENDIX 19: MANHOOD TATTOO

I have not designed the tattoo yet. I want it to look Manly and cool enough that all Men will want to wear it for personal pride and as recognition of being a member of the brotherhood of Men.

I think the Adult & Citizen tattoo will be main tattoo, the biggest, with smaller add-ons for Husband & Father.

BIBLIOGRAPHY

Albert, D., and L. Steinberg. "Judgment and Decision Making in Adolescence." Journal of Research on Adolescence. 21.1 (2011): 211-224. Print.

Belkin, Lisa. "When Is Spanking Child Abuse?." New York Times, Parenting Blog. 21 Oct 2008: n. page. Print. <http://parenting.blogs.nytimes.com/2008/10/21/when-is-spanking-child-abuse/>.

Bennett, William. "Why men are in trouble." CNN Opinion. 04 Oct 2011: n. page. Web. 27 Dec. 2011. <http://www.cnn.com/2011/10/04/opinion/bennett-men-in-trouble/index.html>.

Berscheid, E., and L.A. Peplau. " The Emerging Science Of Relationships." Close relation ships. Ed. H.H. Kelley, et al. New York: W.H. Freeman & Company, 1983. 1-19. Print.

Bogin, Barry; "Why Must I Be a Teenager at All?" New Scientist, p. 34, March 6, 1993.)

Conner, Steve. "Belief and the brain's 'God spot'." The Independent Newspaper. Inde pendent, UK, 10 Mar 2009. Web. 3 Jan 2012. <http://www.independent.co.uk/news/science/belief-and-the-brains-god-spot-1641022.html>.

Council on Families. Department of Health & Human Services.. Marriage in America:. Wash ington D.C.: DHHS, 1995. Web. <http://www.americanvalues.org/html/r-marriage_in_america.html>.

"Definition of Character." Dictionary.Com. Reference.Com, n.d. Web. 9 Feb 2012. <http://dictionary.reference.com/browse/character>.

"Divorce." Wikipedia. Wikimedia Foundation, Inc, 12 Apr 2012. Web. 15 Apr 2012. <http://en.wikipedia.org/wiki/Divorce>.

"Domestic Violence Facts." National Coalition Against Domestic Violence (NCADV). Public Policy Office of the NCADV, Jul 2007. Web. 3 Feb 2012. <http://www.ncadv.org/files/DomesticViolenceFactSheet(National).pdf>.

"Dr. Congo." Amnesty International Report 2009. Amnesty International, 2009. Web. 3 Feb 2012. <http://report2009.amnesty.org/en/regions/africa/democratic-republic-congo>.

Eden, Donna, and David Feinstein. "Energy Medicine for Women." 1st ed. New York: Penguin Group, 2008. Print.

"Father's Day Statistics ." Innocent Dads. InnocentDads.org, 2002. Web. 23 Feb 2012. <http://innocentdads.org/stats.htm>.

Foster, Josh, and Ilan Shrira. "When Parents Play Favorites." Psychology Today. Sussex Publishers, 09 Jan 2009. Web. 9 Mar. 2012. <http://www.psychologytoday.com/blog/the-narcissus-in-all-us/200901/when-parents-play-favorites>.

Gur, Ruben C., Ph.D. Declaration of Ruben C. Gur. Patterson v. Texas. Petition for Writ of Certiorari to US Supreme Court, J. Gary Hart, Counsel. (2002).

"Incarceration in the United States." *Wikipedia*. N.p., 13 Dec 2011. Web. 30 Dec 2011. <http://en.wikipedia.org/wiki/Incarceration_in_the_United_States>.

"It takes a village to raise a child." phdinparenting. PhD in Parenting, 31 Jul 2009. Web. 7 Feb. 2012. <http://www.phdinparenting.com/2009/07/31/it-takes-a-village-to-raise-a-child/>.

Larson, R., and S Wilson. "Adolescence across place and time: Globalization and the changing pathways to adulthood." *Handbook of Adolescent Psychology*. Ed. R. Lerner and Ed. L. Steinberg. New York: Wiley Press, 2004. Print.

Lewis, Robert. "Raising A Modern-Day Knight, A Father's Role In Guiding His Son To Authentic Manhood." 1. Carol Stream, IL: Tyndale House Publishers, 2007. Print.

"Mil Terms B-Bravo." *Combat Magazine*. N.p., n.d. Web. 24 Jan 2012. <http://combat.ws/S4/MILTERMS/MT-B.HTM>

"Mil Terms C-Charlie." Combat Magazine. N.p., n.d. Web. 24 Jan 2012. <http://combat.ws/S4/MILTERMS/MT-C.HTM>.

"Mil Terms S-Sierra." *Combat Magazine*. N.p., n.d. Web. 24 Jan 2012. <http://combat.ws/S4/MILTERMS/MT-S.HTM>

"Protestant Work Ethic, Defined." The American Heritage® New Dictionary of Cultural Literacy. 3rd edition. Published by Houghton Mifflin Company, 2005. Web. 20 Dec 2011. <http://ask.reference.com/related/Protestant Work Ethic>.

"Puberty and Adolescence." Medline Plus. U.S. National Library of Medicine, National Institutes of Health, 10 Nov 2011. Web. 30 Dec 2011. <http://www.nlm.nih.gov/medlineplus/ency/article/001950.htm>.

"Protestant Work Ethic, Defined." The American Heritage® New Dictionary of Cultural Literacy. 3rd edition. Published by Houghton Mifflin Company, 2005. Web. 20 Dec 2011. <http://ask.reference.com/related/Protestant Work Ethic>.

Quigley, Rachel. "What's the Constitution? Don't bother asking 70% of Americans: Alarming number of U.S. citizens don't know basic facts about their own country." Daily Mail (UK). 21 03 2011: n. page. Web. Retrieved 18 Feb 2012. <http://www.dailymail.co.uk/news/article-1368482/How-ignorant-Americans-An-alarming-number-U-S-citizens-dont-know-basic-facts-country.html>.

"Reasons Marriages Fail." Divorce.Com. Divorce.Com, n.d. Web. 15 Apr 2012. <http://www.divorce.com/article/top-10-reasons-marriages-fail>.

"Rite of passage." Collins English Dictionary - Complete & Unabridged 10th Edition. HarperCollins Publishers. 24 Feb. 2012. <Dictionary.com http://dictionary.reference.com/browse/Rite of passage>.

Sagan, Carl. "Chapter 23." Broca's Brain: Reflections on the Romance of Science. Ballan tine Books, 1986. 330. Print.

"Six Pillars of Character, The." CHARACTER COUNTS!" . Josephson Institute, n.d. Web. 9 Feb 2012. <http://charactercounts.org/sixpillars.html>.

Steinberg, L. (2008). "Adolescence". (9 ed., pp. 230-239). New York, NY: McGraw-Hill.

Steinberg, Lawrence. "Adolescent Development and Juvenile Justice, Annual Review Clinical Psychology." Psychology. 2009. 5:47–73 at 54.

Sutton, Robert. The No Asshole Rule. 1st ed. New York: Warner Business Books, 2007. Print.

Tucker-Ladd, Clayton. "Chapter 10: Dating, Love, Marriage and Sex ." Psychological Self-Help. Self-Help Foundation, 2011. Web. 15 Apr 2012. <http://www.psychologicalself help.org/Chapter10/chap10_143.html>.

"Understanding High School Graduation Rates ." There is a Crisis in American Schools. Alliance for Excellent Education, Jul 2006. Web. 3 Feb 2012. <http://www.all4ed.org/publication_material/understanding_HSgradrates>.

Index

T

Again, I want to offer my from-the-heart thank you, and throw out a big salute to all the Men out there who are handling your business as Adults, Citizens, Husbands, and Fathers.

"All a Man expects on Father's Day is the big piece of chicken."
— Chris Rock, American Comedian and Philosopher

Definition of a Man

**"A male who handles all his business,
his duties and responsibilities,
as a mature and responsible adult,
an involved and loyal citizen,
a loving and faithful husband,
and a patient and caring father."**

— William A. "Tony" Lavelle

You notice there is nothing in my definition of a Man as to how tall he must be, nor how long his penis must be? Being a Man is all about good character and a clear understanding of—and the motivation to complete—the four duties of a Man. He can carry out his duties at any height or with any penis size. However, a Man does have a giant set of balls. There is a distinctive ritual within the first Rite-of-Passage ceremony (discussed in chapter 8) as to a Man's sack size. All Men know that part of the ritual very well.

* * * * *

"Personally, I hold that a man,
who deliberately and intelligently takes a pledge
and then breaks it,
forfeits his manhood."
— Mahatma Gandhi

Coming to Gallantry Press

- *Courtship Training Manual--How to Woo Women and Find a Good Wife.*
- *Ladies Guide to Speaking Conversational Martian.*

www.ingramcontent.com/pod-product-compliance
Lightning Source LLC
Chambersburg PA
CBHW050115280326
41933CB00010B/1105